HELP!
MY FACEBOOK ADS SUCK
SECOND EDITION

By Mal & Jill Cooper

MAL & JILL COOPER

eBook ISBN: 978-1-64365-040-1
Print ISBN: 978-1-64365-041-8

Cover Art by Malorie Cooper
Editing by Jen McDonnell, Birds Eye Books

TABLE OF CONTENTS

FOREWORD

Hi, I'm Malorie, and I write a lot of books.

I felt like it was necessary to make that confession before we dive in. Luckily, I'm in good company. My wife, Jill, has written a few more than I, and our collective total comes in at just over two hundred novels and novellas (mostly novels).

If one were to add in short stories and omnibus editions, we would be north of two hundred and fifty.

I bring this up because with all the hard work we put into producing all these books, they need to earn their keep. Jill and I are full-time writers, and whether it's this non-fiction book, or our fiction stories, there's only food on the table if books sell.

Having a plethora of books to market has allowed us to try a number of different tactics, and learn in ways other authors might not be able to—which is one of the reasons we are writing this book.

Our volume of books and commensurate ads also means that if we recommend something here, it works, and we've thoroughly tested it.

A lot has changed since I wrote the first edition of this book just over two years ago, but a lot has also remained the same.

Back then, Jill and I had only seen about a year's solid success from ads, but we knew for certain that ads were the reason we'd sold enough books to write full-time.

We still believe that ads were what propelled us up the ranks, and we've also proved that ads have given us the staying power to weather ups and downs and even a few long gaps between releases.

We also still believe that Facebook is the best ads platform for books, and that it is the best for making good ads that can grab readers and deliver sales—and scale. It's the place where you can become the master of your own destiny.

Throughout this book, I'll note at the beginning of each chapter whether or not the information is new, updated, or unchanged. I feel like even noting something as unchanged is important because we all need to know it is still working the same way as before.

I'd also like to note that while Jill and I both undertook different ads, and wrote different parts of this book, we wanted to write it in the first person—as though it is a casual conversation with one of us speaking to you about how to make your ads better. As a result, we use "I" throughout the book, but it might have been Jill or Mal writing that part or it might have been one of us talking about the other's actions! You'll just never know….

Lastly, there's one thing that *has* changed. If you bought the first edition of this book, the copy you have very likely lists "Michael Cooper" as the author. I'm still the same person, but my name and outward appearance has changed.

Oh! I almost forgot! (I'm not being facetious, I almost did!) We're giving away the digital edition of this book away for *free*, so if you're reading the print version, you can also grab the ebook here: http://www.thewritingwives.com/free-facebook-ads-book.

If you picked the ebook up for free, please consider sending us a payment based how helpful you found it. You can send us a small amount, such as $2 or $3 via PayPal if you so choose.

Optional payment: http://paypal.me/woodenpenpress.

Thank you for your support, and may the ads be ever in your favor.

The Writing Wives,
Malorie & Jill Cooper

MAKING YOUR OWN SUCCESS

Why do I think I have the chops to teach you about this subject?

Before we begin, I want to talk a bit about what success looks like, and why I believe I'm successful enough at Facebook ads to write a book about them.

As I mentioned in the foreword, Facebook ads are the reason Jill and I are full-time writers today, and the reason our books have achieved bestseller ranks on Amazon multiple times and sold over half a million books.

We are neither the most successful authors out there, nor are we the best writers, but together, Jill and I have managed to reach income levels that eclipse salaries I earned working as a software architect and CIO/CTO.

There are well over fifty thousand books coming out each month right now. You've got the storytelling part of the equation down, but no one will see your book unless you get it in front of them. Ads are an integral part of marketing your book and getting it in front of the ever-increasing pool of readers.

The right marketing can give you a second stream of income, and perhaps even major success and the financial freedom that comes with it.

We manage several thousands of dollars in ad spend each month, for our books and the books of other authors. We have a positive ROI on every ad that stays alive for more than 3 days, and we quickly identify ads that don't work, and kill them before they can soak up money.

Success comes from knowing how to craft a good ad, but also from knowing how to spot a lemon and kill it, or figure out how to make lemonade. Success means that you aren't afraid to increase spending on ads, because you understand their performance, and the return you'll get on that investment.

We believe that our success with Facebook (plus AMS, Pinterest, and Instagram ads) gives us the credibility to teach you how to profit with online advertising.

When we note that a tactic worked very well for us, you can be assured that it netted hundreds or thousands of dollars in sales. Conversely, if we say that something did not work, or had only a mediocre return, you'll understand that just making our money back is not what we consider success.

We sincerely hope that you don't take this as bragging but as examples of what we mean when we say that something works and is a viable tactic. We want you to know what success looks like so that you can set achievable goals as you build up your ad repertoire.

With that out of the way, let's get to it, and craft ads that work, while pruning the ones that do not.

TERMS OF THE TRADE

Yes, boring, but necessary. I want to get a few of these terms defined and out of the way, so that when we get into the meat, you'll know what they mean.

CONVERSION

This one is simple. It is the rate at which someone who lands on a page, or sees an ad, performs the desired action.

If it's an ad, then the conversion action is the click-through. If it's your book's page on Amazon, then it's the user clicking the glorious orange "Buy" button.

CPC (Cost per Click)

The CPC of an ad is how much (on average) you pay for a viewer to click the CTA on your ad.

CPM (Cost per Mil)

This is the cost per thousand (not million) impressions on your ad. I recommend that you pay per click, not by CPM, making this a metric you can view on your ad, but not one that has much meaning here.

CTA (Call to Action)

A call to action is the thing that says "Hey, Click Here", or "Yo! Do This Thing!" on your ad or page. It's the "Learn more" or "Like" button on an ad, or the "Buy" button on a page.

Any good promotion (even a flyer you get handed to you) will have a call to action; something that the person handing it to you hopes that you will do.

When the CTA is clicked or followed or taken, that is success.

FUNNEL

Any time there are sales, there is a sales funnel. This is the number of steps it takes to get a customer (in our case, a reader) from first awareness of us as authors, down to the final sale.

Ideally, your funnel should have as few steps as you can get away with. More complex products require longer funnels, but that shouldn't apply to books.

KU "FULL READ"

When I use this term, I am applying it to the full read conversion of a book in KU. That is to say, if the book has 100 KENP, and you get 100 KENP pages read, we assume that is a full read.

Could it be two people reading 50 pages? Certainly; but when we're looking at read-through across multiple books, it's safe to assume that someone who read book 3 read all of books 2 and 1, so the math works out the same.

IMPRESSION

Impressions are, quite simply, human eyeballs looking at a page or ad.

PRODUCT PAGE

Though I speak mostly about Amazon, this applies to all the vendors. The product page is the sell page for your book; if there is a button that starts the process of taking someone's money in exchange for your book, that's the Product Page. For most of us, this will be our book's listing page on Amazon.

READ-THROUGH

The percentage of people who read-through one book and go on to the next, or read-through your entire series.

CUMULATIVE READ-THROUGH

This refers specifically to the people who read-through from the first book to a given book in your series (or to the end, if it's used without specifying the book they read-through to).

BOOK-OVER-BOOK READ-THROUGH

The read-through from one specific book in your series to another.

ROI

This stands for Return on Investment. Ads are investments, and you want a good return on them. Your

ROI is the dollar amount, or percentage, that you make back after spending money on ads.

TRAFFIC

On the internet, "Traffic" is typically synonymous with people's eyeballs looking at a page. In the context of Facebook ads, it means the act of using an ad to drive traffic to a page somewhere on the web (typically, your Amazon product page).

WIDE

A book being "wide" means that it is being sold more places than just Amazon, as in a *wide* number of distribution channels.

PART 1: KNOW YOUR READ-THROUGH

2nd EDITION NOTE: This section is largely unchanged from the first edition (barring some edits for clarity). However, it does contain a bit of information on ACoS for AMS ads near the end.

I'll warn you right away: part one of this book has nothing to do with ads. But if you don't read it and complete the spreadsheet linked at the end, I would not advise running any ads because you'll have no way to tell if they're profitable. Unless you already calculate your read-through, and have your own spreadsheet, of course.

It's unwise to make an investment without being able to calculate the ROI (return on investment). If you don't know what your return is going to be, you don't know if you're sending good money after bad, and flushing it all down the toilet.

In this section, we're going to discuss a series of 5 books, and how to calculate the read-through (RT) of that series, and why this is *very important* when it comes to ads.

I'm not suggesting that you can't run ads for books which are not in a series (either standalone, or loosely connected books), but they are much more difficult to calculate read-through for, and are therefore riskier.

This is mostly because our distributors (read: Amazon) do not give us the tools to know in what order our readers read our books. Without a series, it's very hard to tell how much total profit you will make from the sale of a given book. With a series, you can typically assume that readers start with book 1, and read in order to the end.

The benefit of a series versus standalone books is that you only have to advertise the first book; then you can run it as a loss leader to build your funnel—which is to say you make up the cost of advertising book 1 via the sales of subsequent books in the series.

There are scenarios in which you will advertise books other than the first in a series, but we'll get to that later on.

Now, as defined in the "Terms of the Trade" section, your read-through is, quite simply, how many of your readers read through each book and then pick up the next.

There are two types of read-through: Cumulative, and Book Over Book.

CUMULATIVE READ-THROUGH (CRT)

What does cumulative read-through have to do with ads and ROI, anyway?

The thing we are trying to determine with cumulative read-through (CRT) is the value of a sale of book 1 in your series. In simple terms, you want to be able to say, "If I sell book 1 in my series, I will see x dollars in net profit."

To do this, we need to know how many readers actually make it to the end of our hypothetical 5-book series, what books they drop off on, and how much net profit there is in every book (both on sales and KU reads).

This calculation is super simple for sales. At the end of the month, take all the sales of the last book in the series, and divide it by the sales of the first book in the series.

For example, if book 1 sold 876 copies, and book 5 sold 514 copies:

514 ÷ 876 = 0.5867

59%

This would mean that your entire series has a 59% RT. This is not amazing, but it's not awful either. Based on the authors I've spoken to, this is right down the middle.

To work out the net profits across the entire series, you need to do this for each book in the series (book x divided by book 1).

Don't panic. The end of Part 1 has a link to a spreadsheet that will do all this math for you. All you have to do is plug in your monthly numbers.

If you're in Kindle Unlimited (aka KDP Select), then this is a bit trickier.

NOTE: If you have an omnibus edition that encompasses books 1-3 (for example), or just released the last book in the series, you will see the later numbers sometimes come out to be over 100%. If this is the case, you may be better off using your all-time sales numbers rather than monthly sales.

Another way to deal with omnibus editions is to add the sales number to each book it contains, but divide the KU reads between all three. If the books 1-3 omnibus had 10 sales and 12,000 page reads, add 10 to book 1, 2, and 3, but add only 4,000 page reads to each of those 3 books.

SIMPLE READ-THROUGH EXAMPLE

	Sales	Sales CRT	Reads	Reads CRT
Book 1	100		43000	
Book 2	65	65%	41000	95%
Book 3	50	50%	40500	94%
Book 4	48	48%	39800	93%
Book 5	45	45%	39000	90%

Cumulative Sales RT on the series: 45%
Cumulative Reads RT on the series: 90%

You'll notice that the KU RT is much higher than the sales RT. This mirrors real-world experience (both mine, and many other authors I've spoken to). RT on KU is almost always in the 80% – 90% (or higher) range.

In this hypothetical series, the first book is $0.99, and the subsequent four are $3.99. They have the following KENPC values: 451, 511, 614, 499, 457. KENPC is Kindle Edition Normalized Page Count, which is how many "pages" you can get paid for a user reading if they read the entire book.

If we work out the diminishing cumulative read-through for both sales and reads, and assume a KENP rate of $0.0045, then for every sale of book 1, we make $5.94, and for every borrow of book 1, we make $10.27.

If your book has been picked up by KU readers, and has gained traction there, it is very common to see one borrow for every sale. This means that a sale of your first book nets you $16.21, because every time you sell a book, you (on average) also get a borrow.

These numbers are calculated with the correct royalties and delivery fees, so that is what an actual book's royalties could look like, given the prices and page count stated.

A FUN EXERCISE

Sometimes it's difficult to mentally convert the KU pages read into a number of books borrowed. If you get your KENPC for each book in your series, you can convert pages read to books read, and compare your read volume between KU and sales more accurately.

The spreadsheet linked at the end of Part 1 has a spot for your KENPC, and it will show you full books read if you fill it in.

Here is where you get your **KENPC**:

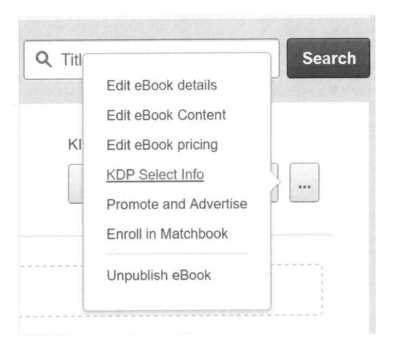

This is displayed at the bottom of the "KDP Info" page for each book in your series.

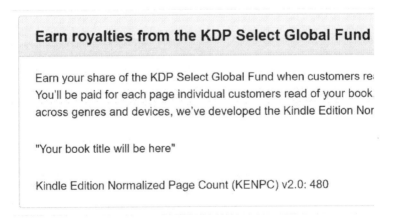

The math here is pretty simple. All you need to do is divide your monthly pages read for a book by that book's KENPC, and you'll have the full reads value.

43000 (pages read) ÷ 451 (KEPNC value)

= 95.34 full reads

Seeing your KU page reads as full books read and comparing them to sales can help you understand the value, or lack thereof, for your books in the program.

Bookreport now supports this as well. You can enable a column named "Borrows" that lists a converted value from KU pages read to an estimate of books read in KU.

On the settings page, set the KENPC full read percent to about 90% to get a more accurate reading.

WARNING SIGNS

If your Sales RT for book 1 to book 2 is below 50%, something is wrong. If your KU book 1 to book 2 TR is below 75%, something is wrong.

By "wrong," I mean something has caused your readers to decide they don't want to carry on. Usually, this means something pissed them off; there's a problem with your writing, or you have a cliffhanger where the main conflict in the story is not resolved.

I should note that you should expect to see very different RT values depending on price. If book 1 is 99c, or free, you will see much lower RT to book 2. If it is full price (ie: the same as the rest of the books in the series), then you should expect a 70%+ RT from book 1 to book 2.

BOOK-OVER-BOOK (BOB) READ-THROUGH (RT)

This type of read-through is less important for ad ROI calculation, but I want to talk about it for a moment, nonetheless.

This is the RT between one book and the next. For example, if you have 45 sales in a given month on book 3 in your series, and 38 sales of book 4, you divide the later book's sales by the earlier book's sales to get your read-through percentage.

$$38 \div 45 = 0.84$$

84%

Therefore, the Book-over-book read-through (BOB RT) between books 3 and 4 is 84%.

That would be a decent RT, but perhaps a bit on the low side this late in the series. Most of the time, folks see RT in the 90% – 95% range later in their series.

Here's an example of a healthy BOB RT:

Book 1 –> Book 2: 50% to 75%
Book 2 –> Book 3: 80% to 95%
Book 3 –> Book 4: 85% to 98%
Book 4 –> Book 5: 90% to 100%

If you see a particular book suddenly fall off a cliff in regards to BOB RT, then you know that you've made a mistake. You probably killed off a beloved character and lost part of your readership.

Chances are, your book's reviews will tell you what you did wrong.

YOUR KENP READS AS FULL BOOK READS

This was a fun little exercise to turn those arbitrary KENP read numbers into something more meaningful. It's also necessary for the next step; but fear not, this is all done by the simple spreadsheet I've provided.

Again, once you have the KENPC number for each book, divide your number of page reads for the month by the KENPC value for that book, and you'll have the number of "full reads" of that book.

Given a KENPC value of 514 for book 1, and a total pages-read of 45833, we would end up with:

$$45833 \div 514$$

$$= 89$$

This means that 89.16 complete read-throughs of book 1 were made.

> *"Wait! You have no way of knowing that those page reads accounted for 89 full reads. It could have been 178 half-reads!"*

If you had the reaction above, you're completely right in your thinking. We don't know this to be true—especially on book 1. However, we don't calculate CRT (cumulative read through) for book 1, so it doesn't really matter that much.

We do know, however, that anyone who reads book 2 likely read all of book 1 – so when we calculate our CRT for book 2 and beyond, we'll still get a meaningful number.

Remember, for KU, we don't get paid by the full read, but rather by each page read. Thus, for our net profit calculations, whether or not someone read the full book doesn't really matter; all that matters is the page-reads volume.

Converting KENP reads to full book numbers is handy because it can tell you the value of KU to you, vis-à-vis how many books in the program your readers are consuming.

Again, fear not, all of this is in the spreadsheet linked at the end of this section.

TRACKING SALES MADE FROM ADS

You can safely assume that all your sales come from your ads, in one form or another—unless you're doing a lot of other promo as well. To know if your ads are working, you need to track sales from those ads. If you're selling no books, this is pretty easy to determine.

However, if you *are* already selling books, and trying out a few different ads, it can be a bit more difficult to know which ones are working.

So how do you tell how many sales come from an ad?

Officially, there is no way to do this. Unofficially, it is possible to get a rough idea via Amazon Affiliate tracking codes. Is this against the terms of service for the Amazon Affiliate program? Yes it is. You are not allowed to use affiliate codes on any service where you bid for keywords (aka Facebook Ads, Twitter Ads, Google Ads, etc…), so do it only at your own risk, and do it only to prove out an ad, and then stop.

If Amazon catches you at this, they will shut down your affiliate account; however, the links you made with it will still work, so it is not the end of the world.

Ideally, you should have different codes for each ad so you can separate your revenue. You can do this by clicking on your email at the top of the page in the affiliate website, and then clicking on "Manage Your Tracking IDs".

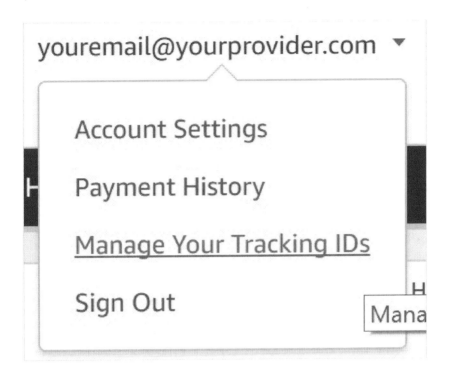

Then, on the following page, you can add new tracking IDs by clicking the "Add Tracking ID" button.

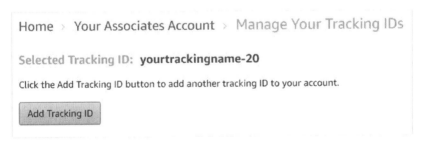

Now whenever you make an ad, you can use the affiliate bar on Amazon to get the appropriate link for your book and ad.

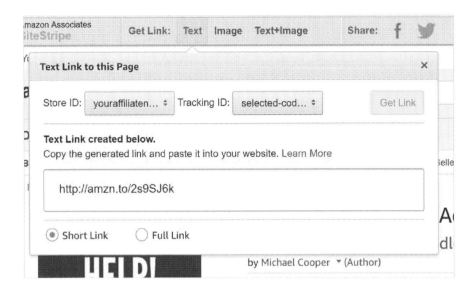

It's important to note that like with AMS ads, there is absolutely no reporting on KU borrows and reads. You will have to assume that the percentage of KU reads you get on average applies to your advertising ROI as well (more on that later).

An aside for any Amazon employee who happens to read this:

We are not using affiliate codes to game the system or make extra money on the side. We are using them because it is the only way we can track the conversions on our ads. We would gladly use a system that didn't pay us affiliate money, but gave us real, useful data on the conversion and effectiveness of our product pages rather than use affiliate codes.

We are begging you for such a service.

TRACKING KINDLE UNLIMITED BORROWS

If you're in KU, you can assume that some number of the people who land on your product page (through your ads, but also through any other means) are KU readers, and invisibly borrow your book.

But how do you track these fine folks?

If some of your ad respondents are reading in KU, then they are a part of your ROI. Well, then. What you need to do is work out the ratio of sales to your full KU book reads.

IMPORTANT: Do not work out this ratio by purely comparing sales earnings to KU earnings.

The reason you should not look at your ratio of KU-reads-to-sales from a dollars perspective is because books like your 99c first in a series will make significantly more in KU. Conversely, your later books at $4.99 will make more from sales (depending on your book's length).

This means that looking at the relationship of KU reads to dollars is not a comparison of actual books read—which is what we need in order to estimate a ratio of humans reading books, as opposed to pages being read.

Since you did the math in the previous section (or filled out the handy-dandy spreadsheet), you can compare your full reads of each book to your sales of each book, and work out the ratio of sales to KU reads, as well as determine how many readers are passing through your series in aggregate.

This is important because you advertise to people, not net profit numbers.

If you have 84 sales and 89 full reads, you add the two numbers together, then divide that number by the KU number to get the percentage of all your full reads.

$$84 + 89 = 173$$
$$89 \div 173 \times 100$$

$$= \textbf{51.4\%}$$

But what we really need is the ratio. To get this, you divide your full KU reads by your sales.

$$89 \div 84$$

$$= \textbf{1.06}$$

This means that for every sale you make, you get 1.06 full KU reads of that book as well.

Because we have little data on KU borrows—where they come from, or how many we have—we can simply assume that a certain percentage of the people who you advertise to, who search for your books or keywords, etc… are just magically "KU readers". We also have to assume that the ratio of "buyers" to "KU readers" is the same, regardless of the route they took to get to your product page.

In the example above, we assume that for every person who lands on your book's product page and hits "Buy," 1.06 people land there and click "Read for Free".

Because this is an average, we can (mostly) safely apply it to our ads, as well. For every sale you see logged in Amazon's affiliate site for a given ad (in this scenario), we'd assume that another 1.06 people also borrowed.

NET PROFIT FROM READ-THROUGH

Let's continue with our example of a 5-book series. We're advertising book 1, and we know that for each sale of book 1, we make $5.94. Also, in theory, a KU reader borrowing book 1 will make us $10.27.

However, I really don't feel comfortable assuming that so many KU readers land on and borrow from my product page. I'm going to pretend that 50% of all KU readers get to my book by magic (as in, Amazon specially promotes KU books to them through an avenue by which it does not promote non-KU books). Therefore, I'm going to cut that $10.27 number in half.

"Wait...what? Why did you just cut your reads revenue in half?"

The base assumption I made is that all readers are equal. If my ratio of buying readers to borrowing readers is 1.06, then I'm assuming it's 1.06 everywhere.

That assumption means that if I am walking down the street and I throw a rock, I'll hit one buying reader, and 1.06 borrowing readers.

But what if Amazon specially promotes KU books to those borrowing readers through some other avenue, and a large percentage of my KU borrows and reads have nothing do with my effort?

I honestly don't know; but to stay safe, that is why I cut my net profit from magical KU readers in half.

OK, back to working out our net profit...

I still multiply the 50% cut of my estimated borrows revenue by the reads KU ratio we worked out in the prior chapter, which means I multiply it by 1.06.

$$10.27 \div 2 \times 1.06$$
$$= \mathbf{\$5.44}$$

And now, for our grand total, a confirmed sale of book 1 in our 5-book series, via an ad, will net us:

5.94 + 5.44

= $11.38

COST OF SALE

Cost of Sale is a common sales and marketing term, and it's pretty straightforward. What does a sale cost you? Hopefully it's less than your net profits on the ad, or you're losing money.

What you will probably find is that about 30 clicks on a Facebook ad result in one sale (give or take 15 clicks). This can vary wildly, and the only way to know for sure is to use affiliate tracking. Again, using affiliate links on Facebook ads is against Amazon's TOS for their affiliate program, so you should only use it for a short time to confirm the ad is converting; even then, know that Amazon may shut down your affiliate account for doing so.

However, this is the only business I've ever been in where you can spend tens of thousands of dollars in advertising for a distributor, but have no insight into the sales funnel. Which is utter garbage.

Anyway, let's assume you see a sale for every 30 clicks on a Facebook ad. This means that the highest cost per click you can tolerate is the result of some simple math. Take your net profit we worked out in the prior section and divide it by 30 (our starting estimate for how many clicks it takes to make a sale).

$$11.38 \div 30$$

$$= \$0.38$$

There you have it. Given our calculated net profit from a sale, and a starting estimation of a sale every 30 clicks, the maximum cost per click we can tolerate is $0.38.

If our average CPC is over that, we're losing money on the ad.

CLICKS AREN'T SALES!

I want to take just a moment to talk about this. I think a lot of people believe that if someone clicks on a link in your ad, or in your newsletter, said click will turn into a sale.

It probably won't.

The conversion rate on your Amazon book page is probably only 2-5%, tops (on average, when you're not running a promo or a new release). When I talk about a sale for every 30 clicks, that is a nice, middle of the road, 3% conversion rate.

Even if you have a great, amazing, rockin' 10% conversion rate, that's only a sale once every 10 clicks.

That conversion rate will also be affected by the price of your book. Free or $0.99 books convert very well. Higher priced books convert at lower percentages.

On the flipside, a lot of people who pick up free books don't read them, and even a lot of $0.99 books don't get read. You will see this reflected in your read-through.

Also, if (in our hypothetical 5-book series) the first book was at $4.99, and our read-through was the same (it would probably be better; the higher-priced your first book is, the more read-through you get), then we make almost $3 more per sale of book 1 in the read-through calculator.

However, your ads will be less effective, and you'll sell fewer books. Like everything in life, it's a trade-off.

A LITTLE ASIDE ON PRICING

The debate on pricing will probably go on forever, and there are as many opinions as there are authors. However, when it comes down to it, there are some key principles at play:

1. People buy things more readily if they are priced lower.
2. People value things more if they spent more money on them.
3. Books that are free, or $0.99, can attract readers who are not your core demographic (because they'll take a chance and buy on a whim, when they may not have at a $3.99 or $4.99 price).
4. Lower priced books often get more bad reviews because of #3 above. Folks that are on the fence about your plot, character, or premise may buy anyway just to give it a

shot. Then they find out it's not their cup of tea, and they give a bad review.

5. You catch more flies with honey. This is to say that, for every single one of us, there is a massive untapped market. I saw the other day that someone did the math on J. K. Rowling, and determined that she had probably only tapped 15% of her target demographic. This means that there are untold *millions* of readers out there for your book who have not yet seen it. They're more likely to see it if it is priced lower, and ranked higher as a result of more sales and borrows.

What do *I* do, you ask?

I price my first at $0.99, because I want *readers* more than money. Readers are great, because if they like you, they give you money!

APPLY READTHROUGH TO AMS ADS ACoS

While this book isn't about AMS ads, the math we do to determine the read-through royalties from follow-on books works for AMS as well.

Once the sheet is filled out, it knows the royalty rate of each book and can work out what profit you make at various ACoS levels.

This makes identifying profitable AMS ads very simple.

AMS	Cost of Sale	Profit (no KU)	Profit (KU incl)
500% ACoS	$ 4.95	$ 7.52	$ 27.96
400% ACoS	$ 3.96	$ 8.51	$ 28.95
300% ACoS	$ 2.97	$ 9.50	$ 29.94
200% ACoS	$ 1.98	$ 10.49	$ 30.93
100% ACoS	$ 0.99	$ 11.48	$ 31.92

READ-THROUGH CALCULATOR SPREADSHEET

OK, that was probably more math than you wanted to do, and math may not be your thing.

To make this simpler and a bit more foolproof, I've created a spreadsheet where you can plug in all your sales numbers for a month, and it will give you your net profits per sale and per read.

You then can add your expected profits together, and divide by how many clicks it takes to make a sale to arrive at your Cost per Click tolerance level.

This spreadsheet will allow you to calculate read-through in a series. There is one tab for a 5-book series, and another tab for a 10-book series. If your series doesn't have those exact numbers, simply input 0 for sales and reads for any books you don't have.

Also, if you have a permafree first book, put in 0 for the royalty rate.

Spreadsheet on Google Docs
(You will need to save or copy it to edit)

Alternatively, the Readerlinks.com service now has a feature based on this work that will also calculate your read-through values.

PART 2: ADVERTISING CAMPAIGNS

2nd EDITION NOTE: This section is largely unchanged from the first edition (barring some edits for clarity).

Gah! "Advertising Campaigns". Doesn't that just sound awful? It's so formal and marketing-y. I should say that I happen to like marketing—especially when I believe in the product. So I hope you understand that I'm not bashing marketers, honest.

Nevertheless, the term just feels so dry!

NOTE: Make sure you set up a Facebook business account before proceeding. This way if your account gets blocked for some reason (such as an ad that violates the rules), it is usually just the business part that is restricted, not your personal account.

Visit https://business.facebook.com to create your account.

QUICK STEPS

(If you're in a huge rush and want to skip part 2)

Go to the Facebook Ad Manager (https://www.facebook.com/adsmanager)

and click "Create Ad".

Pick "Traffic" from the list of campaign types, enter a name other than "Traffic" in the box that appears below (usually your book title), and click "Continue".

Then move on to The Right Audience (Part 3).

OK, that little aside out of the way, let's get into what a marketing campaign in Facebook is, and what it means to you.

A campaign typically encompasses all your efforts to move a particular product down a particular funnel.

In our case, that's usually the first book in a series, and the funnel is three steps:

1. See ad and click
2. Land on Amazon page
3. Buy

Or, if you're advertising for leads (email addresses), which I *strenuously* advise you *not* to, then your funnel is five steps:

1. See ad and click
2. Land on offer (like a Bookfunnel page for your book, or a signup form you manage) and submit.
3. Get marketing email and click
4. Land on Amazon page
5. Buy

Typically, the shorter the funnel, the better it converts.

However, some products (like cars, televisions, computers, expensive enterprise business products) have long funnels because the seller has a lot of explaining, and convincing, to do.

We all know that the full extent of your convincing needs to be cover, blurb, price, and "look inside" snippet. That can all happen on the Amazon product page, so get them there as quickly as possible.

Note: There is a chapter below that spells out exactly why I think that advertising for leads (emails) is bad juju.

And now, as quickly as I can manage, here's the breakdown of the Campaign types we care about, and what they mean.

CAMPAIGN TYPES

When you go into Facebook's Ad Manager interface and click that "Create Ad" button, you're faced with three types of campaigns you can create.

(https://www.facebook.com/ads/manager/account/campaigns)

What's your marketing objective?

Awareness	Consideration	Conversion
Brand awareness	Traffic	Conversions
Reach	Engagement	Product catalog sales
	App installs	Store visits
	Video views	
	Lead generation	

The first pair are in the "Awareness" bucket. These types of ads are for getting likes on a page, or making people aware of your brand. They are aimed more at products sold in brick and mortar stores; things like laundry detergent work well here. Those folks just want to remind people that "Tide Rocks!" so the next time a person is out picking up some detergent, that's the brand they buy. These awareness ads are not terribly effective for us, but they can be used to build up fan pages, which I'll get into later.

The three methods on the right are "Conversion". Now, conversion is really what we want. We want to drive ads to a sell page, and have that bad boy convert. Alas, most of us do not sell our books on our own sites, and these ad types are really geared toward a scenario where you control the shopping experience, and can directly tie an ad click to a confirmed sale and an email address.

Oh, that would be glorious; alas, it is not yet to be for us.

We live in the center column, under "Consideration". In here, there is really just one thing that relates to our goals: Traffic.

What we want to do is drive traffic to our Amazon product page. That page (if you have a good blurb, cover, price, and look inside) should already be a fine-tuned selling machine. If it's not, your conversion rate of ad clicks to sales (once this is all done) will tell you.

The fewer steps there are between the user and that page, the better.

Now I hear you all the way over here. *"I've got this sweet landing page I've made on my website, and it is a thing of beauty!"*

I don't doubt you, but no matter how good you are at making a landing page, Amazon's product page has decades of *science* behind it. It's built to sell. Not only that, but it's familiar to your visitors, and probably more trusted. They like that page. It's where they buy everything, from car parts, to shoes, to groceries. Leverage that.

Also, you have three clicks before users start to get all "meh" about buying anything on the internet. Your ad and the Buy button on Amazon are two of those clicks. If they had to open up the book, or dig into reviews, you've used up another one or two. Do you really want to insert your page on your site in the middle of that?

However, don't take my word for it. When you get your ad built later, do an A/B test, with one ad going to your page first, and another going right to Amazon. Put different affiliate codes on each, and see which way works better.

I'll be right most of the time, but I may be wrong in your case, and I am fully prepared to celebrate your success with you.

Often, people decide to advertise on Facebook for leads. This is a bad idea. The next chapter explains why you really shouldn't do that.

ADVERTISING FOR LEADS

(AKA ADVERTISING FOR EMAIL ADDRESSES)
(aka don't do it)

Let's face it: our books don't really cost that much. We're not selling high-value items here.

This means that the value of an unknown email address is the dollar amount we calculated that a sale of book 1 generates, divided by a rough estimate of how well your Amazon product page converts.

Let's dig into that.

THE MATH ON ADS FOR LEADS

First, you don't get a sale *and* a KU read from someone you're doing targeting marketing at ("targeted marketing" being you have their email, and you are sending them an email directly). You just get one. So take the $5.94 we got for the value of a sale, and the $5.44 for a KU read-through, and average them; that gives us $5.69.

What this means is that if someone whose email address we have takes action on our Amazon product page, and buys or borrows, then we can expect to see $5.69 (again, this is taking drop-off in read-through into account).

There we have it: regarding our single 5-book series, the **maximum** value of a **buying** email address is $5.69. And not everyone buys (as you probably know).

Let's stick with a safe average: one in thirty email addresses buys your book. You may see better than one sale for thirty email addresses, or you may see much, much worse, depending on how you attained those email addresses. So, $5.69 divided by our 3% (1 in 30) product page conversion rate is 17 cents.

There it is. The value of an email address for this series is $0.17. That's it.

> **Again, I know what you're thinking; I can hear it from here.** *"But, Michael, I can get less than 17 cents per click on a Facebook ad for an email address because I tie it to a freebie, and people click like mad!"*

You probably can, yes; I bet I could get the CPC on an offer like that as low as 1 cent per click, if I worked at it.

> **NOTE: Between writing the first edition of this book and now, I tested this theory and found I actually could get clicks down as low as 1c on offers—and they barely converted.**

But here's the rub: your lead generation page (where you send them to get the offer, and where they give you their email address) certainly won't have a 100% conversion rate.

Let's say it has a 25% conversion rate. That means that every four times you pay $0.17 for the Facebook ad click, one person fills out the form to give you their email and redeems your offer. Now that lead just cost you $0.68. And we know, based on our conversion rate of email addresses to people actually buying books (a baseline of 1 in 30), that $0.68 per lead isn't profitable.

Here's the math on that.

Remember we guesstimated our conversion rate on our sales to people when targeting them with a newsletter or other mailing to be one sale per thirty email addresses (again, you can get a real number by using affiliate codes—and you can get authorization from Amazon affiliates to use codes in email). This means that we have to pay $0.68 thirty times over just to make $5.69.

Hint: it's not going to be profitable.

Cost of sale: $0.68 x 30 = $20.40
Value of sale: $5.69

Using ads for leads is not a great use of your money.

You'll find that if you do cross-author promotions (like giveaways, StoryOrigin, or Bookfunnel bundles), you will pay something like $0.01 to $0.03 cents an email. In that scenario, your cost per sale is only $0.90. That turns into a 632% ROI.

SCORE!

This was a very long way of saying that you *generally* shouldn't use Facebook ads for lead generation.

In the "Retargeting" section of this book I will teach you about one way to do this as a part of a wider strategy that does end up making it a more profitable tactic.

Now, I bet there are people out there who have had amazing success doing just what I said not to do, and have built up a list of readers who devour their books. That is *great*, and I don't want to denigrate it, or throw that success into doubt.

What I *do* want to do is give you the tools to know if your investment (advertising for leads *is* an investment) will have a positive return.

Remember, this whole book came out of me being greatly dismayed as I watched authors throw good money after bad at ads and lead generation activities, without getting returns that were worthwhile.

I want you to *know* what sort of returns to expect on your investments, so that you know what "success" means for every activity you perform.

PART 3: THE RIGHT AUDIENCE

2nd EDITION NOTE: This section is largely unchanged from the first edition (barring some edits for clarity).

The topics covered in this section pertain more to basic audience creation and tuning. For more advanced techniques, read the "Audience Layering" section.

If you've been working at this marketing game for a while, or perhaps have been writing to market, then this is not a new topic for you.

Audience is something we as writers think about a lot. Who wants to read our books? Why? What else do they like to read?

What we'll cover here is how to create Facebook's version of an audience, using some of the same tips and tricks you already know, and maybe a few new ones.

Of all the steps in making a good ad, this is the one with the most data, yet it is still a black box. You can easily find groups of people interested in other authors that you *think* are similar to you, but you really have no idea if they'll respond to your ads.

Though we tend to think of them this way, at its heart, your audience is not defined by categories, metrics, or anything other than the type of escapism they prefer to engage in.

If you can figure out what sort of books your audience likes to read, you're in business. If you've written books that *you* like to read, then this part is a breeze: it's probably the contents of your own bookshelf.

SETTING UP THE AUDIENCE IN FACEBOOK'S AD MANAGER

As discussed in the previous section, a campaign is a bucket of "Ad Sets" which are trying to drive a particular type of activity. In our case, this is "Traffic".

If you skipped the chapter above, and are about to click anything other than "Traffic" when creating your campaign, please go back and read it to be certain you understand the implications of your decision.

Before we get to setting up our Audience, we have to make our campaign. Here are the quick steps, once more:

1. Go to the Facebook Ad Manager
2. Click "Create Ad"
3. Pick "Traffic" from the list of campaign types
4. Enter a name other than "Traffic" in the box that appears below (usually your book title)
5. Click "Continue"

THE AD SET

The "Ad Set" is a smaller bucket within the Campaign. We're not yet at the ad level, but Ad Sets contain a number of elements shared by all ads beneath them.

We can't make use of all the options here (such as App), so here are the ones we care about. These are also the only ones we muck with. Default settings are fine for all the other sections.

1. Audience
2. Placements
3. Budget & Schedule

I'm going to work my way up from the bottom here, to get the dull stuff out of the way.

BUDGET & SCHEDULE

A good daily budget to start with is $5. The reason for this is that you don't know if your ad is any good yet, and neither does Facebook. Until you start to prove out that ad, you want to keep your spending low. I get into this a lot more in the "Tuning Ads" section.

Leave all the other settings on their defaults (noted here, in case FB changes the defaults):

- Run ad continuously
- Optimize for Link Clicks
- When you get charged: Link Click
- Delivery type: Standard (there are ways to play with this that we'll get into later)

PLACEMENTS

Here, click "Edit Placements" and leave "All Devices" selected, but open up the "Platforms" section and remove Instagram.

I'm not a fan of mixing Instagram and Facebook ads because often Insta chews up more of the budget with lower conversions. Instagram ads need to be tailored separately, and I cover that in a later section dedicated to them.

THE AUDIENCE ITSELF

Whew! It sure took a bit to get here, but I hope you learned something along the way. This is where we really get into building an actual ad; thus, where the fun starts!

OK, so now we're in the audience section, all you have to type is: "all the people who will love my book".

Jackpot! Print money.

No?

Sadly, there is no magic bullet here, and this little box is the most powerful, and most nuanced part of Facebook advertising. In here, you can build an audience six ways from Sunday, and you can do it wrong more easily than you can do it right.

Let's start from the top, with this idea of a custom audience (which, ultimately, I'm going to suggest you don't use).

CUSTOM AUDIENCES

Facebook knows *a lot* about the people who use it. Seriously, stop telling it your favorite cereals all the time, 'kay? The data gods at Facebook have you all nicely categorized by your likes, dislikes, things that make you tick, and things that blow your stack.

To this end, they can take a group of people (be it people who like your page, or a list of email addresses you import), and find more people *just like them*! Well, then, this seems like the golden gun, the silver bullet, the cat's meow!

Inside the hallowed halls of the Custom Audience, you have two sub-groups. The first is a lookalike audience. These are built from people who have liked you, or a page you run. The other is a custom audience that can be built from Facebook pixel tracking or email lists.

People that you select from a custom audience can still be further reduced or honed by interests, as described in the next chapter

LOOKALIKE AUDIENCE

A lookalike audience is a percentage of a country's (or multiple countries') population that "look like" people who follow your followers.

I have not found these to be terribly effective, and I believe that it's largely because my fans may like a lot of the same things that aren't tied to books. When Facebook builds the audience that looks like them, there may be no readers in there.

This means that you have to constantly outbid all their other interests to get clicks on your ad, and you can end up having very high CPCs.

However, I also believe that you should experiment.

If you have a fan page with over 1k followers and likes, then you can make a pretty good "lookalike" audience. Less than that, and Facebook advises that you may not be able to build a good audience.

To make one of these bad boys, you click the little "Create New" link, and then pick "Look Alike Audience". You can then pick from your pages, and FB will go off and make that audience of people for you to market to.

The defaults are best for your first run, but if you want to experiment with more than 1%, and other options, you should read their explanations.

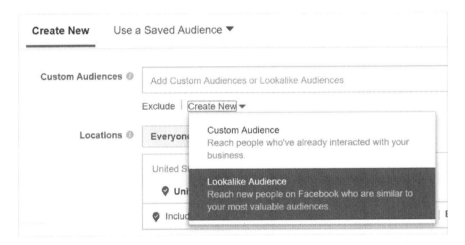

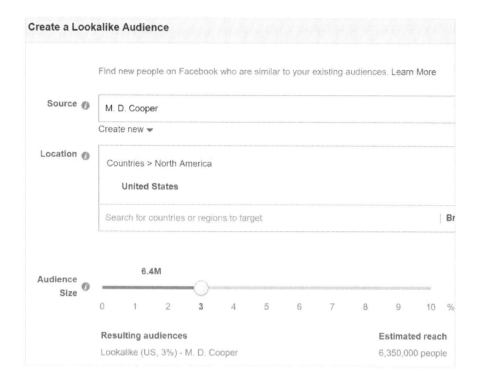

CUSTOM AUDIENCE

Again, these are based on a fixed, known group of people that you provide. They could be from your Facebook pixel, or a mail list you import. You can even hook Facebook up to MailChimp, and it will import a selected list and build a custom audience off that list.

These seem like powerful options that let you build out a group of people to market to.

NOTE: Most of my successful ads don't use audiences based off my email addresses. I use custom audiences based off pixels and

video views. Those topics are covered in
their own sections.

The reason I don't use my mailing list is that I probably already know about these people. I have their email addresses, for Pete's sakes. Why am I paying Facebook to advertise to them, when I can hit them with my newsletter?

Yes I could build a lookalike audience from them, but in general (for me, at least) they don't perform better than lookalike audiences based on my Facebook Pages.

OK, that being said, there is one really good scenario for using an audience based purely on your mailing list, and that is to advertise the next book in a series to people who have probably read the prior book.

Maybe those folks didn't see your email, and you want to boost your read-through. Normally, advertising book 4 to a general audience would not be as effective as advertising book 1, but in this case, you're advertising to your readers for them to read on, and it can help.

There's one other little tricky trick you can use with custom audiences, which I'll talk about when I get to "Social Proof".

The Final Word on Custom Audiences and Lookalike Audiences:

Don't use them until you can build a good audience from targeting alone. They have specific purposes that are often not

conducive to casting a wide net and gathering new readers.

LOCATIONS AND DEMOGRAPHICS

This section is pretty straightforward, but very important to get right. There are pitfalls in here that can eat up *all* your money, and give you nothing in return.

First up is the Country.

Let's be frank; to start with, focus on the U.S. and UK. Other countries don't matter than much (sorry Canada and Australia).

Focusing on Canada and Australia is like spending special effort to market to Florida...well, except that more people live in Florida. I'm Canadian, and I accept this; I know you'll be able to, as well.

EXCEPTION NOTICES

There are always exceptions, right? Well, there are times when it makes a lot of sense to advertise to Canada and Australia.

One is when you have an ad that just isn't doing much in the UK or US anymore. You can just swap it over to one of those countries for a bit.

The other is if you're wide.

Kobo has a huge presence in Canada, and I often run Kobo ads aimed at the Canadian market. Australia has a very strong iBook market, so ads aimed there for that purpose can be very effective as well.

Another scenario is if you have some sort of hyper-regional target for your book. In that case, you'll want to make sure you pick the right place—although, you may find that Facebook ads aren't profitable for that.

I used to also target Germany, but the KU page-read rate there is only $0.0034 now, or something stupid low, so I don't bother (it's fine for German language books, because their words are so freaking long, but English books in Germany suffer because of that low page-reads rate).

WARNING: Whatever you do, *DO NOT* pick India or Philippines. Those folks will like and click your ad to kingdom come, suck up your whole daily budget, and you'll end up with nuffin'.

What I strongly recommend is making a separate ad for the USA and the UK. For now, pick both those countries; when you start getting clicks on your ad, you'll see why you may want to break them apart. We'll get into separating them in a later section.

Next up, pick your age group. I never bother with people under the age of 24—they're broke, and/or don't seem to read. Kidding; they don't seem to read *my* stuff. If you're targeting them, you should, of course, pick them.

Again, we'll get into reading the stats later, and you can see which age groups are most cost effective to market to. For my books, I start my target age range at 25-60 as a safe bet, and usually prune it even smaller once I get stats.

WARNING: MINDSET SHIFT AHEAD

Remember, your marketing targets may not completely align with your main reader demographic. Hypothetically, you could have a huge readership (60% of your readers, for instance) below the age of 20, which probably means that they're not frequent Facebook users—you'll have to target them elsewhere.

However, in this scenario, 40% of your demographic is over 20, and are on Facebook. Well, well! Given population distribution, that's a bigger group of people; potentially in the millions!

So remember, your ad is for a specific subset of your readers, defined by age, location, gender, and interests. The same ad and audience targets will not work for all your readers. Probably not even for 50% of your readers.

The last demographic to consider is gender (referring to Facebook's Male/Female gender selection for ad targeting).

You can't be all things to everyone. You probably know whom you appeal to more, so pick that gender.

If you want to see how you perform with both genders, go for it, but keep an eye on those cost per click stats (again, these will be covered in the tuning section), as you'll find that your ad may cost a lot more with one gender.

OK, THE *REALLY* FUN PART: SELECTING INTERESTS

Now we're at "Detailed Targeting". This is where the meat is (or soy... or cranberries; whatever your jam is).

If you've selected keywords before, this is basically your keywords section, with a twist.

The twist is that Facebook only lets you pick things that have significant fan pages/interest groups on Facebook. You can't select from 99% majority of indie authors, so here you have to pick traditional authors as your targets.

TARGETING BY AUTHOR

The simplest, and most generally applicable way to target is by author name.

You should pick two to six of the biggest traditional author names who write books just like yours. And by "just like yours," I mean their covers and blurbs look close to yours, in addition to the content of the book.

There's a ton of nuance here, and it's different per genre. I strongly recommend Chris Fox's book, "Write to Market". Even if you didn't write to market (or the idea is abhorrent to you), the same selection principles will apply for ad targeting.

When we get to ad tuning, we're going to get into how to tweak these interests and learn from your mistakes, as well as learn how to get the most for your ad dollar.

TARGETING BY GENRE INTERESTS

A genre interest is something that relates to your genre, but not specifically to books. A good example is if you were to type in "Romance". You're going to see a lot of options, and some may be a more general interest, but most are going to be actual fan pages/groups on Facebook.

A group that comes up when you type "Romance" could be about a specific movie, or even a broader target, like romantic songs, that may contain a lot of non-readers (though this *can* be adjusted for, and I'll get to that). Luckily, for Romance, there is a "novels" interest, so that should tell you that they're readers.

Another common genre target are TV shows and movies.

I write Science Fiction, and so you'd think that *Star Wars* would be a great target for me, right?

Wrong.

A grillion people are also advertising to *Star Wars* fans, and they're willing to pay more per ad click than I am. Also, there are probably a lot of non-readers in there.

However, Timothy Zahn is a traditionally published author who just (at the time of the first edition writing) wrote a new *Star Wars* book about Admiral Thrawn.

Ooooh, now *he* would make a good target. Excuse me for a moment. ;)

So, you can use movies, TV shows, and other genre interests (and I often do), but be judicious and do your best to keep them on target.

WORD OF WARNING

A quick piece of advice is that if your cost-per-click is *super* high, then you are probably bidding for expensive keywords against a lot of other people. You may need to move down to a midlist author for your targeting, or remove any broad genre interests (like games, tv shows, or movies).

GET A GOOD AUDIENCE SIZE

As soon as you narrow down an age and gender, and pick a country (in my case: US men, 24-65+), you'll see a population count. That group is about 83 million people, from the looks of it. This makes sense; there is a pretty reasonable number of men in the U.S. in that age group who are on Facebook. But all the 24+ year-old men in the U.S. is a little general. Facebook's little meter is (understandably) pointed over at "Broad".

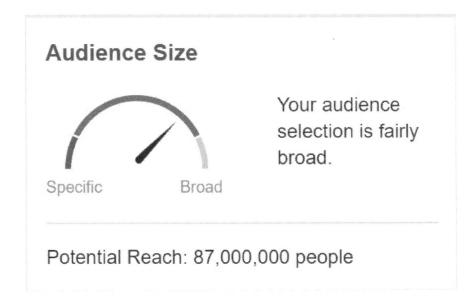

In the section above, I talk about picking your interests; what I didn't get into is that spiffy little audience size count that shows as you hover over the interests. This puppy is a big deal.

If you type in a keyword like "Sci-Fi," you'll see some interests with millions of people, and others with seven. Be sure to pick the interests that actually have people interested in them (unlike the example below).

I try to add interests and authors till I get close to a million in total.

Once you've gathered a decent group of interests for your audience, a little link will appear below this box with an option to "Narrow" the audience. Click that and add "Amazon Kindle".

What you've done here is said, "Facebook, target all those people that like *ANY* of those interests in the first section, *AND* like Amazon Kindle" (which hopefully means they read on one).

You can experiment here, and add other variations of the Kindle interest, but *keep it just to Kindle!*

Even if you're wide, I recommend this. All the ads in this Ad Set target the same group, so you don't want to show ads to people who read on iBook or Google Play, and then send them to Amazon.

Once you get a good Amazon ad rolling, duplicate the Ad Set and make an audience that targets your other platforms. This will also help you track your ad ROI per platform.

CONNECTIONS
Oh ho! What do we have here?

In this section, you can target, or exclude, people who like me, my pages, etc....

When I first create a new ad, I often limit it to people who like my page. I want them to give me the "Social Proof" (aka likes, comments, shares) for the first few days, and then I go back and edit my audience and *exclude* them. No need to advertise to people who have already bought my book.

A FINAL TRICK

Let's be honest, guys can be a bit more…well, rude, in the comments they leave on ads than women tend to be. It's often not intentional; men frequently speak bluntly and without non-verbal cues to see how their tone is taken, and can come off as brusque.

However, men tend to curb that behavior when women are present. Yay for socialization! (I have no idea if I'm being sarcastic or not…)

This can work to your advantage. If you're advertising to men, pop into your reader group and ask the women to comment on an ad after you put it up. That helps your Social Proof, and also will cause men who come afterward to leave better comments.

SAVE YOUR AUDIENCE

Seriously. Save it. Whether it's good or bad, you want to remember these selections (especially if the audience doesn't work out—no need to target those folks again).

PART 4: CRAFTING THE AD

2ⁿᵈ EDITION NOTE: This section has substantial changes to reflect new features and options that Facebook has added in the past few years.

OK, I lied before; *this* is the fun part!

Once you've created, and saved, your Ad Set (which is where audience, placement, and daily budget all live), we get to the heart of things: the Ad itself.

There are a number of ad types you can make, but I'm going to start by telling you which ones *not* to do.

I know, I'm such a Debbie Downer, aren't I?

Don't do a video, carousel, or collection.

The reason is not because they don't work; it's that they're either expensive or time-consuming to create (or both). No one gets all their ads right on the first run, and every ad needs some tweaking. It's often cost prohibitive to tweak a video ad, and carousel and slideshow ads have a lot of variables.

I do toy with them from time to time, and I'm getting better at them, but even at their best, they don't convert as well as my single image ads.

ANATOMY OF THE AD

Single image ads have five parts:

1. The top blurb above the image (Primary Text)
2. The image
3. The headline text
4. The description below the image.
5. The URL/Link

These five parts make for a lot less to play with when you're tuning the ad (than the other ad types, that is), and a lot less to have to put together when you're making it.

TIPS FOR IMAGE FORMATTING

A bit further down, I'll talk about how to pick a good image, but here I want to just add some notes about how to get the best out of your image.

Facebook now lets you have different images for different locations. You can either upload three separate images, or crop one.

Start by picking the image and uploading it.

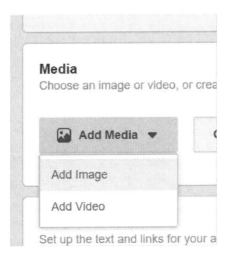

Once it's uploaded, toggle the slider in the "Recommended Aspect Ratios" section.

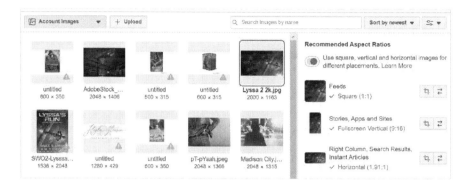

Then crop your image so that it will look good at each aspect ratio.

Becomes…

The majority of ads are seen on mobile devices, and a square image takes up almost 2x the screen real estate on mobile, so square is now *highly* recommended. Also, it will cause an ad to work much better on Instagram (more on this in the "Instagram" section).

THE MEAT AND POTATOES

I mean…unless you're vegan. Then it's veggie meat. Trust me.

This interface has changed a bit and contains some really cool new parts. But first, we need to talk basics, and because I just like to be crazy, I'm going to go through these sections in almost no particular order.

Because reasons….

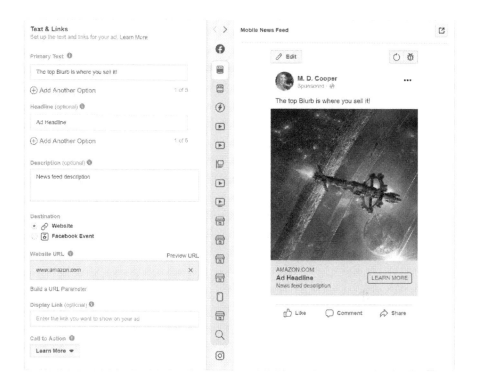

WHERE TO LINK YOUR AD (Website URL)

Before we get to how to craft that ad, let's talk about where to link it. Previously, in the section on not using ads for lead generation (email address capturing), I talk about the reasons you should always link your ads directly to Amazon.

In case you skipped that part, I really want to reiterate it here.

Remember the funnel. You want that funnel to be as short as possible (while still enticing the reader to buy). Essentially, this means the fewer steps, the better.

Getting that reader right to the Amazon product page, which is purpose-built to sell, is your number one goal. You should already have put significant effort behind a good cover, catchy blurb, and a good, grabbing peek inside; that being said, there are a few scenarios where you *might* want to send people to a page other than your Amazon product page.

1. You are advertising a multi-author promotion or giveaway. In this case, that page is your destination page. It's where the "sale" happens.
2. You are running some discount on multiple books.

I did this recently, where I discounted three books in a series. To facilitate that, I ran single ads that landed the reader on a page that listed all three books with links to get them on sale.

OK, so now that we have that out of the way....

THE TOP BLURB (Primary Text)

The Facebook interface refers to this simply as the "Text". This is the section above the image, which I often refer to as "the blurb".

There are two ways to write this blurb. The first is to write it as "you," and the second is to write it as a marketer. The "you" version will be long, and should bring out your passion about the story. The marketer version should be about the deal, ratings, reviews, awards, etc.

MARKETER'S VERSION

This one comes in two flavors. The first one is what I call the "Pimpin'" ad. Here you're flashing pedigree, reviews, a great price; you're pimpin' that puppy out.

PIMPIN' EXAMPLE

> BOOKNAME *by AUTHOR is rated as one of the best GENRE books out there. Top reviewer, NAME, said it lit his pants on fire! NYT Best-selling AUTHOR is bringing his/her/its A-Game, and you don't want to miss out!*

The Pimpin' version is best suited for sales and deals, because then people really just care about quick facts and savings. "Get *BOOK* by AUTHOR this week only, for just 99c! Critics love it and rave…."

You get the picture.

I find that this type of blurb does not work for a long-running ad, and puts off a lot of readers (though it works for some).

CHALLENGE EXAMPLE

> *Is Malorie Cooper the next J. K. Rowling? Pick up a copy and find out for yourself!*

Well that's pretty bold, isn't it? Some people may not be comfortable doing an ad like this, but they can really work. Just be prepared to police ad comments as the jerks show up.

That being said, Facebook doesn't really care that much if comments are positive or negative. If people are engaging, the platform thinks your ad has value to their audience, and they show it more. Any comments are social proof.

Also, look at the stats for how many people chose not to have that ad, or any of your ads, shown to them again (which we'll get to in the tuning section), as you do want to make sure you're not putting people off too much.

YOUR VERSION

This one comes in a number of flavors. The first one is the "Flat-Out You" version.

FLAT-OUT YOU EXAMPLE

Hey, folks! I hope you don't mind me taking this little bit of your Facebook news feed, but I wanted to tell you about my latest book that is fan-freaking-tastic. It has dragons, an evil wizard, and a young lad who has to beat all the odds. I wrote it in an LSD-fueled haze, and it was amazeballs (the LSD and the book). You're gonna love it.

This type of copy works best when you're making ads for people who have liked your page, or people who really have a close set of interests to your book.

These people already know you and your voice, and will respond well to it. Also, they are often just in need of a small reminder that your next book is out and waiting for them to devour.

These ads have the benefit of being genuine, which a lot of people really like and respond well to.

PLOT-BASED EXAMPLE

> *Dragons rule the land, and no one is safe. Even those who do attempt to venture out of their holds in defiance of the dragons find themselves attacked by the evil wizard. One young man possesses the power to defeat all the bad guys and save the day!*

This is the type of ad that people always tell you not to make. They tell you to make the marketer's ad. But for most authors, that's just not who we are; we're storytellers. That's our jam.

I say we should embrace that.

Our readers come to us for stories. What better way than to get that story across to them in the ad? Tell them about the grand adventure that awaits them, of swordplay, or love, or desperate times!

You (should) have a strong emotional attachment to your book and know why you love it. This is a strength. Use it.

When you're done writing this ad, read it aloud in a movie announcer voice. If it doesn't make you want to rush to the theater to see it on the big screen, keep working till it does.

CHARACTER-BASED BLURB

Jimmy has lived all his life in the Grimlock hold, scraping by to get food and shelter, and survive the daily rain of dragon poop. But one day, through some amazing circumstance, Jimmy discovers that he has a stupendous destiny to save the world (plus the girl — if she doesn't save him first)!

The character-based blurb is really just a twist on the plot-based one. There's a reason for this: some people prefer character-driven stories, and other people prefer plot-driven stories.

Chances are that your story is both. So make an ad for each element and run both. What you'll find is that about ¾ of the time, your plot-driven ads will resonate better with men, and character-based ads will resonate better with women.

That's not to say that women don't like plots, and men don't like characters. It's just that gender is a fairly clear marker as to a *preference* for one over the other.

However, experimentation is key. Disparate demographics, markets, and genres will yield different results.

I had an ad that I was *certain* would not appeal to women, and so, for five months, I only targeted it at men. Then, as I began to saturate that audience, I decided to duplicate the Ad Set (since that's where the audience is contained), add one reference to the main character in the story, and put that ad in front of women.

And it did great! It cost about $0.10 more per click than it did for men, but it was still within my tolerance for a positive ROI, and I reached a brand new audience with the ad.

THE FUN AD EXAMPLE

Who doesn't like to have a bit of fun?

Right after Jimmy finishes his after-school snack, he's gotta go save the world — or at least his town.

That is, if his mom doesn't make him clean his room first.

He'd better get to it, or plant-eating zombies are gonna be everywhere!

Ads like this really pair well with funny and food-related images. People also usually engage with them more; and the more engagement your ad gets, the less Facebook charges you for your clicks.

Obviously, you can't do this for a tragic book. But if your story has humorous elements, you can certainly pick out a few and make a fun ad that shows off your book's character.

THE *RIGHT* IMAGE

Stop right there! I saw you grabbing your book's cover to make a little banner image. I know what you think you're doing, and you can stop it right now!

I'm going to start with the don'ts for you again.

1. No book covers
2. No slices of your book cover (like a horizontal slice that you cropped out)
3. No text of any sort

There may be an exception to this rule, but it only applies to people who are willing to pay $1.50 per click, and I haven't experimented with it enough yet. When I do, I'll let my FB Ads mailing list know how it turned out.

I can hear you again; you have a ream of reasons as to why your book cover will be the perfect thing for an ad. Let me explain to you why it's not: *Facebook* doesn't like it.

The good folks at Facebook have long-since determined that advertising images with words on them piss off their users (because, let's be honest, most people don't really *like* ads). Users who are pissed off from seeing crappy ads need to be shown fewer ads, or they leave the platform.

Facebook doesn't want people to leave just because they're inundated with market-y ads all the time, but they want to make money selling ad space. The result? They don't want your ad to look like an ad.

You're readying your response, aren't you?

"But, Malorie, FB now allows text on ads. I have several of them running right now!"

Yes, you may have, but my experience tells me that your ad with text on the image may be shown *less*, and cost *more* per click than the exact same ad with no text on the image.

I test this about once a month. I did it again just a few days before writing this segment, and it still holds true.

I took two ads in the same Ad Set, identical in every other way, and ran them side-by-side. The one with the text showed about only one fifth as often, and cost over three times as much. This was even *after* I requested a manual review of the ad, so that it wouldn't have the display restrictions for being text-heavy.

WELL, WHAT IMAGE SHOULD I USE?
Great question, glad you asked it.

After I did my initial posts on Facebook advertising, this is one of the questions I got asked most frequently.

Previously, I mentioned that you shouldn't slice off a chunk of your book cover and use that. You're probably wondering why; you paid a lot of coin for that gal-darn cover, after all.

The reason is that the framing of the image on the cover often won't work if you take only a slice.

In art, there are concepts like negative space, and the placement of main elements in the image and their relationship to one another. Also, some people feel uncomfortable if they see a picture of a person with the top of their head cut off. Finally, color balance may be wonky on a narrow slice of your cover image.

A good image that was specifically composed to have a balance of elements across a landscape (wide) image will be built differently, and will simply work much better.

The best thing to use is a straight-up stock image. You can get subscriptions on major stock image sites, like depositphotos.com, and snatch up good pictures that fit your genre.

Important Consideration:

These images don't really need to match your book. They need to match the *genre*, and they need to have good contrast to grab the eye on a Facebook feed.

I know this will really strike some of you as hard to believe, but trust me. I have spoken with many, many authors who spend as much as six figures on Facebook ads each year. This is how they do it: stock images, no text.

Plain and simple.

A FINAL WORD TO THE WISE ON IMAGES

I ran an ad, at one point, for a science fiction series. The image featured a girl standing on a ship, staring out over a starscape. You saw her from the back, with her head turned to the side ever so slightly. Great image, worked well with both men and women.

From the waist up, it looked very proper and not like something anyone would have an issue with. However, from the waist down, she only had thong coverage of her bum. It honestly bugged me, and I still might pay a digital artist to put pants on her, because it's a striking image.

So, I uploaded the image, and used the cropping tool in the ad manager to show her only from the waist up. I submitted the ad, it was approved, and I started getting clicks for a good price.

Then I started getting weird comments on the ad such as, "Well, nice picture, but I'll read it for the STORY," and others like that. I didn't think much of it; people leave weird comments all the time.

Then, not too long ago, I used the image again, flipped through the different preview modes, and made a rather interesting discovery.

If you don't do it yourself manually, Facebook crops the image differently for different placements (sidebar, Instagram, audience network, etc). There she was, with her butt hanging out on half those placements…

Intellectually, I knew that the Instagram and mobile images are tall, and crop differently, but I hadn't ever uploaded an image before when I didn't want a specific part of it to show, so I didn't think to check how it would appear.

So, if there is a part of an image you don't want to show (be it booty, or even just an element that doesn't fit with your story), crop it the way you want on your computer *first*, before you upload it to Facebook's ad manager.

SAMPLE IMAGES

Just some ideas to get your creative juices flowing. These images are all licensed from Depositphotos.com and Dreamstime.com. Only use royalty-free images licensed from a reputable site.

THE AD HEADLINE

Chances are that if you have already entered the link to your book, FB has auto-filled the headline and the "News Feed Link Description" fields.

Don't use these defaults.

Make your headline snappy. Make it plot- or character- or deal-based.

- *"Only 99 cents for a limited time!"*
- *"Save the dragon hold, save the world!"*
- *"Jimmy has just one chance at redemption!"*

This headline should be the punch that follows your blurb above the image. It's your big do-or-die sell line, but it also needs to stand on its own.

Now, over in the center of the page, there's an ad preview section with little images. If you hover your mouse over it, you can see the different ways your ad will look. Flip through these options to make sure your headline isn't cut off at a weird spot on some of those formats.

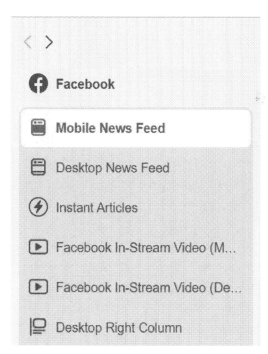

NEWS FEED LINK DESCRIPTION

This is smaller text that goes below the headline, which does not show up in all ad placements (you can cycle through the preview options I mentioned above to see it). A lot of the time what I use this for is to provide the yin to my blurb's yang.

If my blurb is all "raw me" marketing, then I put some character or plot stuff down there. "See what Tanis will be up against as she takes out the big bad and saves the day!"

If it's a character or plot blurb, I might put, "M. D. Cooper is an NYT best-selling author who loves kittens, and has been compared to Isaac Asimov and Larry Niven."

That's a bit short, but still preview it to make sure that on the formats that *do* show it, it's not cut off in a weird spot.

Again, don't be afraid to be funny in your ads if it fits with your books (which it should, if your characters are real, and are not in exceedingly sad situations all the time).

BUT WAIT! WHAT IS THIS SORCERY?

You can now do multivariant testing without having to make special campaigns to test more than one ad type. This is useful if you have an image you know works, but really want to hone your text.

Note: Multivariant testing is like A/B testing, but there are more than just two static options. In this case, you can put in up to five different headlines and blurbs, and Facebook will mix and match them to find the best one.

Ideally, unless you have a high spend, you don't want to do too many. If you have 5 of each, that will create 25 combinations, and it will take some time for all 25 to show to enough people for the ad system to decide which is working best.

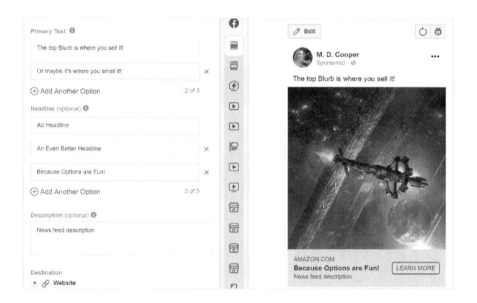

YOUR AD IS COMPLETE!

OK, it's not actually complete. First, you need to pick your call to action button. I really wish there was one that said, "BUY!" but there isn't. I vacillate between "Download" and "Learn More".

The effectiveness of one button text over the other probably has more to do with the ad copy than anything else. Feel free to experiment.

But before you submit it, here's one last thing to consider:

SHAMELESS SELF-PROMOTION

No, not for me; for you. That's what ads are. You are promoting yourself, and that can feel damn awkward. On the flipside, the folks who do a lot of marketing tend to *forget* that it is *supposed* to be damn awkward.

The more you advertise and promote, the more you start to think of yourself and your books as a brand. You detach yourself from it all and treat it like not-you. That is OK, and it's natural. I'm sure there's even some name for it.

But be careful. Your readers don't see you that way.

They see self-promotion as a bit distasteful, and they like authors because they feel like they're making a connection with a human telling them a story.

You need to keep this in mind as you make your ads.

Self-promotion works best if it's "raw you" talking right to the reader, or if it's a deal. They don't care if you're shamelessly pimping yourself if they get a bargain in the mix! ;)

PAY NO ATTENTION TO THE MAN BEHIND THE CURTAIN!
There is a way to have the best of both worlds, and it is to not run your ads as you. People will respond to a recommendation from a 3rd party far better than they do to one from you directly. This is obvious; this is why we do NL

swaps, and use paid book services. It's why reviews matter, and why social proof is huge.

So how do you do it for your FB ads?

Here's the deal. You have your author page where you talk to your folks, push your deals and wares, and post snippets and cover reveals. This is you. Run your "raw you" ads from this page. Don't run your market-y/plot/character ads from this page, because they aren't coming from "you".

What you need to do (and this will take time, a *good bit* of time) is make a new genre fan page. If it's SF, you could make it about a trope, or maybe about some good books or TV series. If it's UF, you could make a Buffy fan page, or a general genre page like "Great Romance books I Love".

Run your ads as that page. Pimp other people's books there (good books that you believe in), and you'll build trust with folks who like and follow the page. That way, when you promote *your* book on this page, people will trust you and they'll check it out.

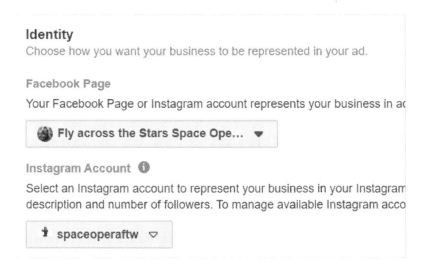

Keep in mind, though, you need to run that page as a faceless marketer. It only works if you create a marketing persona for yourself, and run the genre/fan page as them. Some people can't do that. If that's the case, work out a way where you can run it more as "you," but you'll lose some of the advantage of the "trusted recommender" promoting your books.

Do not pay for likes, or run giveaways to build followers on this page. You want this page to be true lovers of what you're putting up there. As you run ads as this page, you will get people liking the page. I know; crazy, right? People will click "like" on the sponsor of an ad!

It does take a year or so to build up a genre-based fan page organically (at least, it did for me). But when it's built, it will be just as powerful as a newsletter, and will give you an additional marketing and promotion avenue.

SUBMIT THAT AD!

OK, we're ready to submit the ad, so go forth and do it.

Some things to remember (and to double-check, which you can do by clicking along the list of steps on the left side of the page):

1. Budget should be set to $5
2. Don't do Instagram unless you have already nailed Facebook
3. Pick a country
4. Pick a gender
5. Write copy like you're a human, not a marketing robot
6. **No book covers on your ad's image**
7. **No text on your ad's image**

8. Remember what *you* love about your work, and sell the emotion

Seriously, if you don't listen to any other advice I have, do #6 and #7. You will see better results. Guaranteed.

Your ad will take a bit to get approved (though it's faster when there's no text in the image), and then once it has, the stats can have a few hours' delay.

What we're doing at this point is seeing how the ad resonates with your market. If you have a killer ad, you'll know this in one day. You may also have a fantastic ad that will take 2 days to prove out. Expect to spend $10-$15 for each ad you test. If you're on day three, and the ad isn't picking up steam, then it's time to axe it.

"So, how do I really know if my ad is working?"

Read on, gentle reader, read on…

But first, here are some of my ads for you to check out:

A colony ships leaves Sol at the height of Terran civilization; taking with it the greatest, most valuable technology humanity has ever created. It is destined for 82 Eridani, where the colonists plan to build a new life for themselves.

The ship never arrives. Centuries slip by, then millennia. Five thousand years later, the ship returns—its abilities and power greater than when it left. It is the most coveted treasure in the galaxy, and the deadliest weapon ever imagined.

The Lost Colony Ship

In the spirit of great Space Opera by Peter F Hamilton, Jack Campbell, and Larry Niven comes Aeon 14. If you love strong heroines like Kris Longknife, then you're going to love Tanis Richards. Major Richards needs to get out of the Sol…

AMAZON.COM   **Learn More**

2.2K Reactions 184 Comments 386 Shares

Lara Crane stopped the rewind agency from controlling time, and hasn't used her own time travel abilities in years.

But that's about to change.

Someone she never expected has a little bit of revenge planned for her. revenge that is going to undo much everything she's ever worked for.

Seriously Twisty Time Travel Plot

If you can't handle twists and turns, stay away from Jill Cooper's 15 Minutes and The Bridge series. They'll melt your brain!

AMAZON.COM   **Learn More**

Major Tanis Richards will be up against the toughest challenges of her life. Not that she's worried, what with the Marines of Bravo Company at her back.

Outsystem: A Military Science Fiction Epic

In the 42nd century, the greatest colony ship ever built is leaving Earth...In the spirit of great Space Opera by Peter F Hamilton, Alastair Reynolds, Jack Campbell, and Larry Niven comes Aeon 14. If you love strong heroines like Kris Longknife and...

AMAZON.COM   **Download**

251 Reactions 28 Comments 43 Shares

M. D. Cooper
Written by Michael Cooper [?] · September 9 · 🌐

⋯

A WOMAN OF STEEL WITH A HEART OF GOLD.

Rika is one of my favorite characters I've ever written. She's a woman who I admire and am continually impressed by. Yes, she's a person I made up, but she really has a life of her own and she reflects the experiences of a number of women whose efforts have brought her to life.

Let me tell you about her...

Rika's story is that of a girl who was falsely accused of a crime she didn't commit at age 18. She was given a choice: life in prison or join the military. After agreeing to conscription, she was turned into a cyborg warrior against her will.

Then it got worse. Her side lost the war and she was left with a body she hates and no one left who cares if she lives or dies.

Despite that gloomy start, this is a story about hope and love and finding a new family. It's about building yourself up by choosing to do the right things, even when they're impossibly difficult, and to believe in the good inside those around you.

Dive into military sci-fi with a heart. Join Rika and her Marauders.

https://amzn.to/2PRUyIV

i About this website

AMAZON.COM

Rika Outcast - A girl whose armored heart will ensnare you

Download

PART 5: TUNING THE AD

2nd EDITION NOTE: This section has some changes surrounding relevancy, but is otherwise largely unchanged from the first edition.

Before I get into tuning the ad, I want to talk about failure.

I used to work as a software architect, and the one thing we worked hard at was detecting failure—and doing it as quickly as possible. We weren't just looking for errors in programming, but also in our thinking. A slogan we adopted was "fail fast".

The same thing is true in ads. You aren't going to make a perfect ad the first time around. Or the second, or the third. Just like your writing, this is a craft that you have to hone and continuously improve.

Also, most of us writers are great at long-form writing, and terrible at short-form. It's just not something we do that often. That's why I'm a believer in the story ad; an ad that highlights your story and your storytelling abilities.

What "fail fast" means for us, is that you need to constantly look for ads that aren't working, as much as the ones that are. Also, *every ad will eventually stop working,* so failure is a state that every ad will reach at some point.

SPENDING MONEY

The other thing you need to think about is how much capital you can invest in ads before you see a return.

Let's look at a moderately successful scenario:

You're running ads at $5/day, and your first three all flop. Each of those flops took three days to prove out as failures. That means you've spent $45 on failure. This is OK! Note what didn't work, and don't do that again. But ad #4 is ticking and getting you clicks at a good CPC, and sales are coming in.

Keep in mind that sales can lag by days, in some cases, so if you see clicks on day one and two, and sales in KDP reporting don't yet match up with affiliate reporting, don't panic right away.

Because you're not made of money, you keep ad #4 at $5/day for two months. That's how long you'll have to wait, give or take a bit, until Amazon is going to pay you for those sales that you made when your ad started to roll.

At this point, you've fronted $300 on ads. Can you tolerate that sort of spending until you get a return? Be aware of that delay, and plan for it.

You can also pause an ad and start it back up again. You don't lose your social proof, though FB may charge you more per click for a bit.

OK, so failure costs you $45, and success costs you another $300. That's a good baseline to start with.

RELEVANCY – THE MOST IMPORTANT METRIC

NOTE: Facebook said about a year back that relevancy would be gone by now, and that it would be replaced by three new metrics. They brought the new ones in, but they seem flaky (sometimes not populating) and Relevancy is still here. I'll address the new metrics in the next section below.

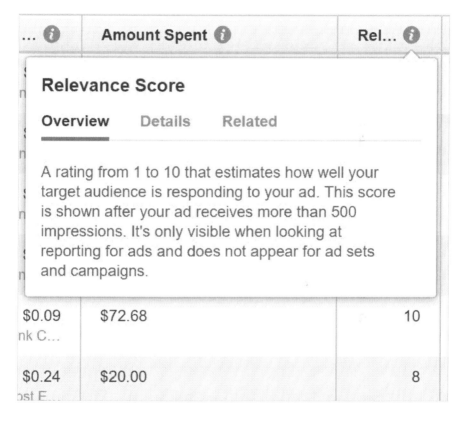

Relevancy is how relevant Facebook believes the ad you've made is to the audience you've picked. What Facebook doesn't want is someone targeting 50-year-old male bikers with tween dresses. It's a waste of everyone's time and money, and it devalues Facebook's platform, so they want to put a stop to that by hitting biker-targeting tween dressmakers in the wallet.

Don't be a biker-targeting tween dressmaker.

Facebook's goal is to show ads that blend well with newsfeeds. Those ads should contain words and images that people *like* seeing because they're interesting, funny, informative, and spot-on with a reader's likes and dislikes.

To this end, Facebook gives your ad a relevancy score once it's been shown 485 times. This score is on a scale of 1-10. The lower the score, the less Facebook will show your ad, and the more they'll charge to do it. I shoot for a 10 out of 10 score, but I'll live with anything down to an 8.

If my relevancy is under 8, I start tweaking and tuning that ad.

THE NEW RELEVANCY – SORT OF IMPORTANT TOO?

The new relevancy metrics are Quality Ranking, Engagement Rate Ranking, and Conversion Rate Ranking.

Quality Ranking ▾ Ad Relevance ...	Engagement Rate Ranking Ad Relevance Di...	Conversion Rate Ranking Ad Relevance Di...
Above average	Above average	Above average

Essentially what they've done is taken the old score and broken it down into three metrics. Let's take a quick dive.

QUALITY RANKING

This is the "perceived quality" of your ad. The two things that affect this score is if people tell Facebook they don't like your ad (reporting it in some fashion, or marking that they don't want to see ads from you anymore) or if the page you link to takes too long to load.

ENGAGEMENT RATE RANKING

Engagement is how much people "do stuff" with your ad. This means clicking on the art, the link, liking, sharing, commenting, etc.... It's based on a ratio of how many times your ad gets shown to how often these actions are taken.

CONVERSION RATE RANKING

Simply put, how often people click on your ad. It's reflective of how many impressions to clicks you get.

NOTE: These three metrics are compared against other ads being run on Facebook that target the same audiences. They're not purely objective measures.

There are five ratings you can get:

- Above Average
- Average
- Below average (Bottom 35% of ads)
- Below average (Bottom 20% of ads)
- Below average (Bottom 10% of ads)

Your ad needs to be Above Average or Average. Consider Average to be a relevancy of 7-8, and Above Average to be 9-10.

WHEN TO TUNE THE AD

The easy answer to this is: always. All ads will eventually lose effectiveness, and you want to have your next, well-performing ad ready to go. I even keep a few old ads warm so that I can turn them back on if my current batch starts to lose steam.

However, what you're really looking for are the signs that an ad isn't working.

The first, as mentioned above, is relevancy. Shoot for 8 and above.

Second is the CPC. This will start high and move down; if you have a good relevancy and result rate, then this will usually trend in a good direction. If it doesn't come under your tolerance level, then you need to tune the ad.

**Your tolerance level's something we determined using the ROI spreadsheet. You filled out the spreadsheet, right? Don't make me send you a facepalm gif. I'll hunt you down and do it.

The last sign is the result rate. This is effectively the percentage of clicks or interactions you get per impression. If it's below 2.5%, then the ad just isn't performing; you're showing it to a lot of people and they're just passing it by.

There are some smaller factors, like your frequency (which has to do with audience saturation), but that's something we can go over another time.

YOUR AD'S FIRST FEW DAYS OF LIFE

Before we get into how to tweak your ad, I want to take just a moment to talk about its early days and what you should expect. I'm doing this because I don't want you to panic and mess up what could be a great ad.

A HIGH COST PER CLICK

The cost per click (CPC) on an ad is the *average* of what you paid to have someone click on the ad.

I could have an ad that displays a $0.30 CPC, but there could be dozens of clicks that cost me over $1 in there, and others as low as 1 cent. Sometimes a bunch of those expensive clicks happen at the outset of your ad, and there aren't cheap clicks to balance them out.

You're going to see a high cost per click at the outset. Only ads that are *amazing* home runs start off with low CPCs.

Part of this is because you pay more for clicks before you have a relevancy/engagement score. Again, this is because Facebook wants to show relevant ads. In straight dollar click bidding, whoever is willing to pay more to show their ad wins and gets the impression; this is how AMS ads work, for example. Highest bid on the keyword gets displayed.

Here's an example:

I have a huge budget for an ad, but a relevancy of 5 or a below-average engagement. You have a small budget (which means Facebook has less $ to spend when bidding), but your relevancy is 10 and engagement scores for your ad are above average. All other things being equal, Facebook will show your ad over mine, and you won't have to outbid me to do it.

That's because your relevancy/engagement score is a part of the bid.

So, because your youthful little ad does not have a relevancy/engagement score yet, it's bidding for clicks at a disadvantage, and you pay more. This will trend down as your ad gets more social proof and, eventually, relevancy and engagement scores.

What you should expect to see is an ad that levels out in the $0.10 - $0.30 CPC range by its third day. It may fluctuate after that, but chances are that you can't afford a $0.39+ CPC.

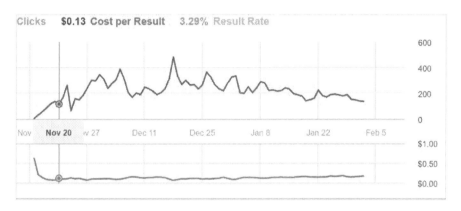

TWEAKING AD COPY VS. TWEAKING AUDIENCE

These are the main two elements that are going to affect performance. Essentially, are you showing the right ad to the right people?

Maybe it's the right people and the wrong ad; or the wrong ad to the right people; or maybe both are not lining up.

How do you fix one without breaking something that may be working just fine?

IT'S NOT ME, IT'S YOU

If your relevancy is high (8+) and your engagement is above average, but you're paying a bundle for clicks, then there is typically an audience issue.

AUDIENCE IS TOO SMALL

Go back and look at your audience size; the number shown may be smaller than Facebook said it was when you first built the audience. That happens sometimes. You may also see the little meter pointing over at the "Narrow" side.

Try to add some more interests, or maybe remove (or make a bigger) "lookalike audience," if you used one of those.

I recently had an ad that I knew should work. Copy was catchy (made *me* want to buy the book), and the image had performed very well in the past, but I couldn't get the CPC below $1.50 (choke).

I looked back at the audience, and realized that I had used a lookalike audience that had somehow reduced my total pool down to a thousand people. In this scenario, Facebook couldn't find any low dollar targets, and had to bid my ad high to get it to show to these people.

I took out the "lookalike" part and resubmitted it, and now it's settling down around $0.20 per click.

OVERSATURATED AUDIENCE

When you did your interest targeting, you may have picked the tippity-top authors in your genre/category; so did everyone else when they made their ads.

Now, if your offer is good, like a freebie or some deep discount, you may be able to target those top authors, and have things work like a dream.

However, maybe you have another ad that you want to leave up so that it makes a few sales a day. That ad may do a lot better if you go down to some mid-listers in your category, or if you dig into some sub-categories, and target authors who do well in certain niches.

When you do this, you may need to pick a few more authors to get a good audience size, but if it's a slow-burn ad, you may be okay with audience sizes even down to 10,000.

Another option is to pick some authors of yesteryear. I often pick a lot of SF greats from the days of yore. They cost less to target, but still have nice big interest groups.

Science Fiction examples of this are people like Anne McCaffrey, Robert Heinlein, and Arthur C. Clarke.

A great way to find these authors is to think of who was big when you were younger, or browse the stacks at the bookstore.

NOPE, TURNS OUT IT'S ME AFTER ALL

On the flipside, if your relevancy and engagement are poor, then you've produced an ad that your chosen audience isn't interested in. If you're certain that your audience is spot-on, then it's time to play with the ad and not the audience.

Another indicator of this scenario is good relevancy/engagement, but a low result rate (below 2.5%). In this case, people don't mind your ad; they may be liking it, even commenting on it, but they're just not clicking.

So, let's get into tuning your ad copy and image.

TESTING OUT AD CHANGES

No one has a crystal ball (well, I do, but it's in need of repairs, on account of it not working), and no one knows for sure which ads will work best.

There are thousands of variables that can affect how well your ad is going to work. However, you don't have time (or patience, or money) to test thousands of variables. Even testing five or six different variables (multivariate testing) becomes exponential very fast. For example, if you have two sets of five variables, you have 25 possible combinations to test.

Nuts! Ain't *nobody* got time for that!

This is where multivariate testing's little brother, A/B testing, comes into play.

Here, you take a SWAG (scientific, wild-assed guess) at the biggest variable, and try two versions of the ad with that biggest variable being different.

I'll give you a hint: That biggest variable is invariably the image.

The image is going to make or break your ad before anyone reads a single word of it, so that's what we want to twiddle with.

STOP!

Before you go one step further, I need to tell you what happens when you change an ad.

It loses all comments, shares, and likes.

That's right; if you change the image or any of the text in an Ad, all your social proof goes *poof!*

You can, however, change the audience on the ad set—though changing the audience will nuke your relevancy/engagement score, and you'll have to rebuild it.

You used to be able to change the link without losing social proof, but that is no longer the case.

OK, you may proceed.

DUPE THAT AD!

So, now that you have that ad made and approved, mouse over it, and click that little "Duplicate" link. This will allow you to make a copy of the ad.

In this new copy of your ad, you only change *one* thing (again, if your ad isn't working, try the image first), and then save it.

If you want, you can run both versions of the ad simultaneously; though you may need to up the budget in your ad set (remember, all ads in the same ad set work off the same budget), so that the other ad shows often enough to get relevancy/engagement scores in a reasonable amount of time.

You can also pause the first version of the ad and let the new version run on its own for a bit—though there could be time of day/week/month variables that come into play, so these results may be skewed if you're not running the ads at the same time.

Sometimes, Facebook decides that one version of your ad just isn't something it wants to show, as compared to another version, so it just doesn't display it much. I've had this happen with images that did very well on other ads. What I do then is duplicate the entire ad set so that the version I want to test has its own dedicated budget.

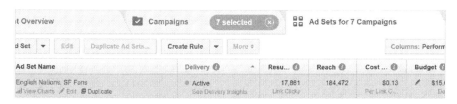

You may also want to tweak the copy, because you're on a tight budget, and trying out a dozen images is expensive. It doesn't hurt to do this (especially on an ad that just isn't working), and you could strike gold. Just remember to give your new copy a couple of days to see how it shakes out.

DUPING FOR FUN AND PROFIT

Not every image appeals to everyone. We're all different (thank goodness, eh?), and different things appeal to each of us.

I often keep two or three copies of an ad running with different images, if they're all working. Something else I do is prove out several versions of an ad with different images, but then turn some off and rotate them, so that I'm not hitting people with the same stuff all the time.

DEMOGRAPHICS AND PERFORMANCE

As you've certainly picked up by now, I'm big on knowing whether or not something is working. I believe that knowing when something is *not* working is the most important of the two.

We only have so much time, money, and effort available to us in life, so we need to spend as little of all three on things that don't work.

Luckily, Facebook gives us oodles of information to help find out what's not working.

DEMOGRAPHICS

We can view demographics for an entire ad set, or just for an ad. Because we really care if a given ad is working, let's look at the demographics for a single ad.

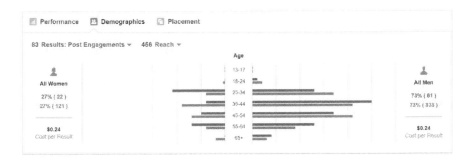

Click the "View graphs" link, and then click the "Demographics" link. What you'll see is a breakdown of men vs. women, and then impressions to clicks for each age group.

As you scroll down through the age groups, you can see what their individual costs are. You may find that certain gender/age group combinations are too expensive; you can go back to your audience and exclude them.

You may also find that you have odd mixes, like an ad that works well with women 40+, but with men 20+. What I do in those cases is duplicate the ad set so I can target my best male/female age groups separately. I also often take that opportunity to tweak the image or text to be more appealing to each gender.

RESULT RATE

While you're in here, if you click the "Performance" tab, you'll see your result rate and cost per click per day. This is a useful graph for seeing where your ad is trending from a cost perspective. The thing you want to keep an eye on is the Result Rate. Ideally, it should be above 2.5%; a decent ad will be in the 4 – 6% range. A great ad is 10% and up.

One thing that is annoying is that that the result rate isn't per day; it's over the entire date range you have selected in the upper right. Be sure that when you're evaluating an ad's performance, you are looking at just the prior seven days or so, and then comparing it to the ad's lifetime performance.

BREAK IT DOWN!

No, it's not dancing time; at least, not yet. We're going to head into some deeper data here about how your ad is performing.

When you're on the Ad, or Ad Set tab, there's this handy-dandy "Breakdown" button.

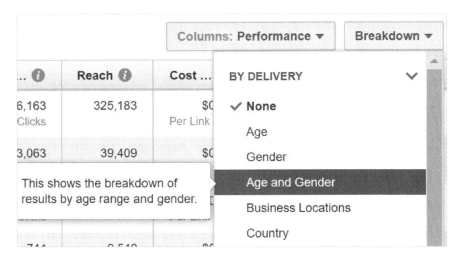

You can see there a lot of different ways to slice and dice the breakdown, all the way down to the state they live in, and the time at which people interact with the ad.

Some of this is duplicative of what you can find on the graphs and charts, so you can choose how you prefer to consume the data.

I find the breakdown handy for spotting outliers across all my ads. I can look at all my CPCs in one big view, and see the age/gender groups that are breaking the bank. I can also see the ones that are cheap and interacting.

Some other things in here are the impressions, clicks, and cost per click by time zone.

If you look at it for your time zone, what you may find is that there are certain times of day where you can get more eyeballs on your ads for less money. For me, on the East Coast, that usually starts at about 8:00 – 10:00 PM.

So here's a little trick, nestled deep in this book for those of you who get this far: every night, at around 6:00 – 8:00 PM, I increase the spend on my best ads. Not by a lot; if I have an ad with a daily budget of $15, I might adjust it to $20, or if it's $35, I might bump it up to $42. Then, come morning, I lower them back down.

You may be thinking,

"Dear God! I don't have that kind of time;
this girl spends at least an hour a day on
her ads!"

Maybe not an hour, but some days, yes, I do. My ads are the lifeblood of my sales. When Amazon's algorithms stop favoring a new book, I can keep it going with ads. Often, when Amazon's algorithms see a product page of mine that is converting well, they too will promote that product, so ads can drive more sales straight from Amazon. And my ads, even ones operating at a low level, serve keep you up in the ranks.

To that end, I try to squeeze every drop of performance from my ads that I can.

PART 6: NURTURING THAT GOOD AD

2nd EDITION NOTE: This section is largely unchanged from the first edition (barring some edits for clarity).

At the end, there is information on using the same ad in more than one ad set without duplicating the ad in order to retain Social Proof.

After you've done all the hard work getting that ad tuned and performing well, you want it to keep on chugging, and maybe even get better and better, right?

Right?

I thought so. Sure, you can keep a little ad trickling along at $5/day and help keep a series afloat. I've run some ads for folks with that spend, and they can keep a series with a $0.99 first book at about the 30,000 – 50,000 rank range with ease.

Now that's not too bad. If your series is five books long, and you have good read-through, that rank-range means you're probably making $20-$40 a day (if you're in KU). Even if only $10 a day of that is coming from ads, you're doubling your money every day.

Very few investments will yield returns like that.

But let's see if we can turn that knob up to 11, shall we?

MANAGING YOUR AD SPEND

You've diligently run your ad at $5/day to get that nice relevancy/engagement score, some shares and comments, and to settle into a good CPC. Now it's time to bump that spend up and get some magic happening!

Not so fast!

Here's the thing you need to consider: the audience you picked is only so big. At a higher spend rate, your ad may saturate that audience, and Facebook may start charging you a lot more per click because people start hiding your ad, or ignoring it.

You can see this as the frequency score on your ad. Close to 1 is good; if you're over 1.5, you're starting to saturate the audience.

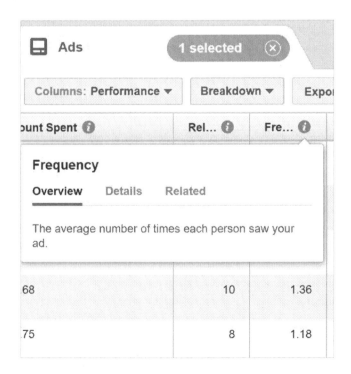

NOTE: You should look at a one to two-week range when gauging your frequency. All of the numbers shown when you're looking at an ad are based on the date range selected in the upper right of the page.

Because of this, it's best to up your ad spend by a few dollars every couple of days, as you fish out the sweet spot. I've found that with a lot of ads, you hit a point where you'll start to see that CPC begin to climb. It's often around $30-50 per day.

"Why does this happen?"

Even if an audience is listed as being in the millions, not all of those users are on Facebook at once. Some might only log in once every week or so.

Others may have the interests you've selected, but other interests as well, such as computers and cars, and ads for those products command a higher CPC and earn Facebook more money. This is why your ads may start to see their frequency climb when you haven't come close to showing them to the entire audience.

However, if you up your spend sufficiently, Facebook will start showing it to people who cost more to put ads in front of, and that is why your CPC will start to climb.

In a nutshell, with a higher daily budget, you chew through the low-hanging fruit faster.

When you get to that point with an ad, it's time to start a new one and start warming it up, so that when your current heavyweight ad begins to lose effectiveness, you can boost the new ad up.

I often have situations where one ad is on the way up, and another ad is on the way down, in terms of spend.

Also, if you read the end of Part 5, then you even know what time of day you should be doing that nice little incremental bump in spend.

SOCIAL PROOF

The Internet is awash with algorithms that try to determine whether or not humans will like a given thing. However, none of them are as good as *actual* humans for deciding what humans like.

To that end, Facebook still wants to know if actual people like a post. This is your "social proof".

Social proof on Facebook consists of likes, shares, and comments. The more likes, shares, and comments a post or ad has, the more social proof it has. Higher social proof means more relevancy, and FB will show it more, and charge you less for clicks.

In case you missed it before, Facebook does not do an all-out bidding war based on what you're willing to pay. There are people who will bid more for placement (or have more budget), but lose to you if you have a lower bid, but more social proof on your ad.

You can look at a long-running ad and see cost per click go down when you get comments and shares on your ad (likes affect this as well, to a lesser extent).

Part of why I bring this up is to temper excessive duplication of ads. While I encourage it so that you can hit specific groups of people with more targeted content, be sure that you don't spread your social proof too thin.

Keep this in mind as you build out more ads, especially on a limited budget when you're running multiple ads in an Ad Set.

A TRICK TO IMPROVE SOCIAL PROOF

As I've mentioned before, you can change the audience on an ad and not remove the likes, shares, or comments on that ad. This means an audience change doesn't lose your social proof.

Something I often do with ads is run them for the first few days targeted at my fans, and friends of my fans. Then, once I get good relevancy/engagement scores, some comments, likes, and shares, I alter my audience to *exclude* my fans.

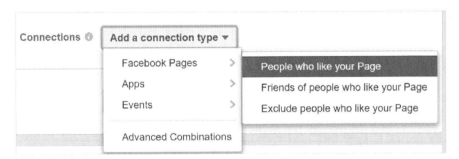

COMMENTS

Previously, in one of the locations where I spoke about social proof, I mentioned that Facebook (by and large) considers all comments to be good comments. A healthy debate between two people (even if there is negativity and disagreement) is good business when your product is the discourse.

To that end, even "This book sucks poo poo" is a comment that boosts social proof for your ad. That being said, you really don't want that on your ad, do you?

What I do to comments like that is hide them, and let them live in their little echo chamber. Sometimes I hide them but still respond (if the comment isn't too antagonistic).

However, just like you need a few 1-3-star reviews on your book, some lemon comments don't really hurt you much, either. In fact, they may help.

Right now, I'm running a challenge ad where I ask, "Is M. D. Cooper the next Larry Niven?" (for non-SF nerds, Larry Niven has been a Science Fiction titan since the early 70s).

That's a pretty tall order. I don't think I'm as good as Larry Niven, even on my best day. However, it has sparked some fun comments.

Some I've hidden, but others I've engaged with, and we've discussed the merits of his books and mine. Some comments had people saying that his stuff sucked and mine was great.

That being said, don't run challenge ads under your own Facebook author page. Those need to live under one of your fan/genre pages so that you can address the comments with your marketing/publicist hat on.

Also, just like 1-star reviews (yes, I respond to many of those), if that comment has burned your cookies, give it a day and see if it still bugs you enough to reply to it.

Whatever you do, don't get antagonistic with folks. Your readers are seeing your ads too, and they won't be happy if you come off like an ass.

PRODUCT PAGE TWEAKS

This is just a final little note that may help your product page convert just a bit better.

You're bound to have a particular ad that is your *main* ad at any given time. It may be character, plot, or even deal related. You want that ad to have a good flow into your product page so that the reader feels continuity.

To that end, what I recommend is for you to add a bit of text at the top of your blurb that connects your ad to the rest of your blurb.

For example, my book blurbs on my product pages are almost always character-based (talking about my main character and her challenges), but my best performing ad was plot-based, and the first paragraph of the blurb bore little resemblance to the ad.

To remedy this, I added in a bold paragraph that was a good grab line, and also connected to the ad.

This one change boosted my ad's conversion rate by 20%.

THE DEATH OF YOUR AD

All good ads go to heaven, so it's OK to kill that ad when its relevancy/engagement wanes, its CPC starts to climb, or its result rate diminishes.

I suspect you won't have too much trouble killing off dead ads, since they hit you in the wallet. However, those ads that ran long and did well can have a second life.

Take a look at the demographics you selected (be it gender, country, or age), and see if you can tweak the ad and give it new life by hitting a new demographic.

I recently had an ad that ran from November to May, and was finally getting to the end of its life. However, I looked at it and saw that I had made a silly mistake that caused it to have never shown in the UK.

The mistake: I used a lookalike audience that was US-only as the foundation of the Ad Set audience.

Well, well, well, I thought to myself, as I rubbed my hands together and quickly duplicated that ad with a UK-only target. Sure enough, there was this massive group of people across the pond that loved my ad.

That book has since moved from an average ranking of 12,000 to about 2500 in the UK store as a result. This book had been as high as 400 in the US store, but even then, its UK peak was 2400.

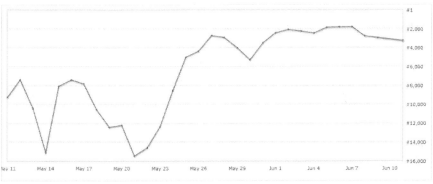

UK Sales Rank over the month. Down a bit now, which means I need to look at my audience saturation, but it's quite the jump!

That one little glance at a dying ad put a 5-year-old book into the top 2000 in the UK store.

Another option (which I also undertook) was to take the ad and retool its copy to be more character-based. Previously, that ad had bombed with women; but with this retooling, it did well (not amazing, but well), and has probably sold about 400 books at this point.

GET THAT AD DOING DOUBLE DUTY

While the standard creation process has you make new ads to put in ad sets, you can also take existing ads and put them into a *second* ad set.

What this means is you can have a single ad that you show to men, women, USA, and UK, but rather than lumping all those demographics into one audience, you can make multiple ad sets to capture those audiences with different budgets while serving them the same ad.

This is a great way to take an ad that's working well and has has good Social Proof, and leverage it further.

To do this, choose the "Use Existing Post" option when creating an ad.

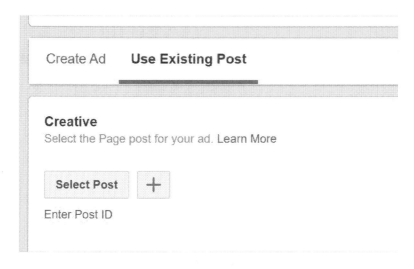

Then click "Select Post" and pick the ad, or even post on your page the one you wish to use.

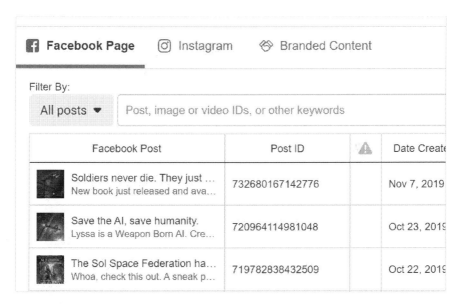

Once you pick an existing ad, the existing creative (image, text, etc…) will be used, along with the social proof.

Remember, in this case, it's not a new ad, it's two ad sets using the same ad, so if you do change something on the original, it will edit what is shown on the other ad set as well.

PART 7: AUDIENCE LAYERING

2ⁿᵈ EDITION NOTE: This section is entirely new!

In the audience-building section, I introduced you to a two-layer audience. We put our interests in one section and then used the "Narrow Audience" option to focus in on people who read books.

Now it's time to take this a step further, once we talk about whether or not low CPC is really the best metric by which to gauge ads.

THE LOW CPC MYTH

This is not a cut and dried topic, because tracking conversions on Amazon is *very* difficult. However, let's assume we are using affiliate links, and that they are a good barometer of conversions.

I've done experiments where I have gotten the CPC for an ad down as low as 1 cent per click. I did it by creating super-generic audiences and ad copy that would appeal broadly. This particular ad averaged closer to 3c, but it did dip down to 1c every so often for a day or so.

It converted terribly.

Let's face it, if you made an ad that said, "Click here for a free pony," people would click that thing all day long. But will they buy your book when that's the Amazon product page they land on?

Probably not. So it's fair to say that low CPC isn't everything.

Let's do a little bit of math to prove this out. I'm sorry, it'll be quick.

Let's say that we have a CPC of $0.10 (10 cents), and a conversion of 1 in 50. That means it costs $5.00 to make a sale.

$0.10 x 50

= $5.00

Now, what if we had a $0.25 (25 cents) cost per click and a conversion of 1 in 20?

$0.25 x 20

= $5.00

Well now, that's the same cost to sell the book you're advertising! Which means that with a total read-through value of $25 (from our 5-book sample series at the beginning of the book), we make the same profit.

Now, what if we have an ad that costs a bit more, but converts at a rate of 1 in 10?

$0.30 x 10

$$= \$3.00$$

Now we're spending $2.00 less to make a sale, and that's going to add up. What if those people were more likely to be superfans? If so, they'll have higher readthrough than average, and you'll turn an even higher profit.

SUPERFANS

When you write a book, there are people out there for whom it is the *exact* sort of story they want to read. You nail their demographic and interests perfectly, and they'll gobble up everything you have.

Of course, the real question is how to find them.

Let's take a hypothetical example. Let's say that I have written an adventure thriller that I know Clive Cussler's readers will love. I hit all the tropes, my writing is tight but easy to read, and I have a fun and witty style.

If I were to make an ad targeting people who like Clive Cussler and a bunch of other thriller authors, I might just get people who watched the movie Sahara and then picked up a single Clive Cussler book. They're not guaranteed to be huge readers, and they might never buy a book for which they didn't first see a movie version.

They might be potential superfans, they might not.

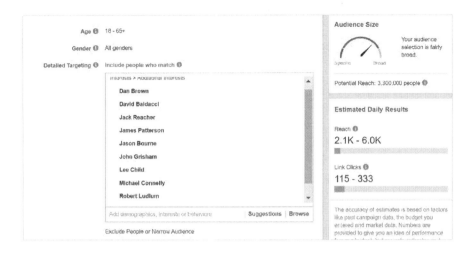

We see here that I have an audience of about 3.3 million people. With a $20/day spend, I can reach quite a few of them.

Now, let me add in my audience-narrowing e-book interests.

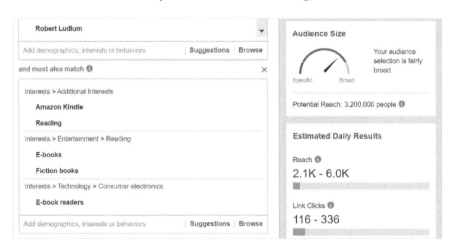

Here we have an audience of 3.2 million, pretty much the same as before. Looks like this demographic (at least the ones on Facebook) read a lot digitally.

The low-end of the link click estimate of 116 clicks (at a $20/day spend) means it would cost $0.17 per click, which is a decent number. I'd have to have a CPC of around $0.06 per click to get 336 a day, and I doubt that would happen— though it's nice that Facebook thinks that highly of my skills.

The thing is, this audience contains everyone who likes just one of those authors/characters and happens to read books. But what happens if we layer that audience and look for superfans?

MAKING THE LAYER

Alas, it's not layer cake, but it's easier than layer cake, and might make you a lot more money, and then you can buy a lot of cake.

OK, I have no idea where I was going with that, but hopefully it was worth a laugh.

Let's take that group of authors and characters and split it in three.

These are the same authors with the same e-book/fiction interests in the mix. We'll see that we went from 3.2 million people down to 62,000. However, we know that these people have picked up more than just one author's books, and that means there's a better chance that they'll pick up mine.

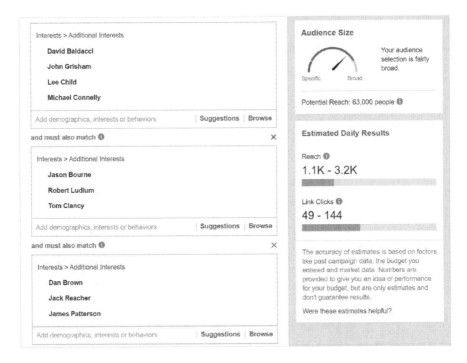

Let's take that low-ball number of 49 clicks for my $20 daily spend. That comes out to $0.40 cents per click. That's some serious scratch per click.

If we say we want a baseline of no more than $5 to sell book 1, then we need to have an ad that converts at about 12.5 to 1. That's not impossible, and if it gets you a superfan that gobbles up all your books, it will pay for itself in spades.

But let's see if we can sweeten the pot a bit by adding more authors.

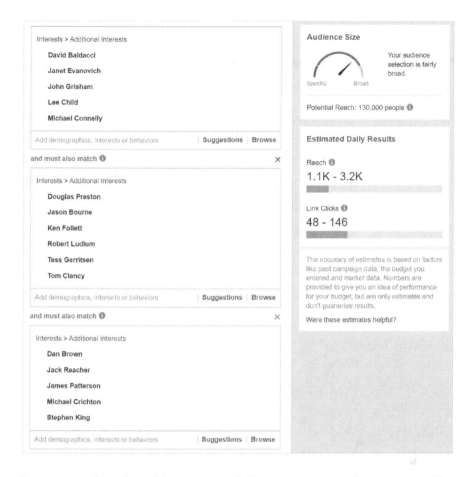

Interestingly, in this case adding more authors actually lowered my estimates, but not by any meaningful amount. I did, however, double my pool of readers. So long as these authors all still align well with what I've written—so that I can deliver on the promise I'm making to my readers—I should be able to draw them in well.

Of note, when I do target expansion, I can roughly double this number, and that might yield good results, but it also might reduce the number of superfans I attract.

Another option that does not see you slaving over keywords, trying to find interests that are actually on Facebook, is to use interest-generating software.

There are a number of them out there; alas, none are cheap. Usually in the $200-$500 price range, often including subscriptions as well. I've tried a few, and my experience has been that they aren't much better than I could manage myself with about 10-15 minutes of effort.

Essentially, I was underwhelmed.

On top of that, I know my market very well, and building audiences isn't something I do very often. The cost benefit analysis tells me that I'm better off doing it myself.

I suspect that if you run a business doing ads, software like Connectio would be worth the cost, but otherwise, not so much.

PART 8: VIDEO ADS

2nd EDITION NOTE: This section is entirely new!

Video ads on Facebook have two purposes: one for direct action (sending people to buy your book), and one for building an audience of people who engage with your content.

Firstly, I'll go over how to make a video ad, and what sort of content you want to put into your video. Then, in Part 10, I'll discuss how to leverage people who watch your video to show them more ads in the future.

MAKING YOUR OWN VIDEO WITH FACEBOOK'S TOOLS

Shortly after I wrote the initial version of this book, Facebook released some tools to dynamically make your own videos out of static images.

Frankly, they kinda sucked. However, they've really come a long way. Now you can upload up to 6 images, and the video creation tool will give you a number of options, some even seasonal.

To begin, click the "Create Video" button in the ad creation page.

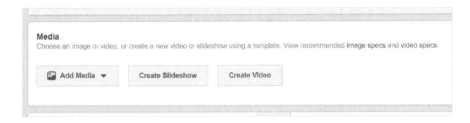

Once the new window opens, you can upload 1-6 images to create a variety of videos with custom text overlays.

The great thing with these is that you can easily make square videos that are idea for mobile placement.

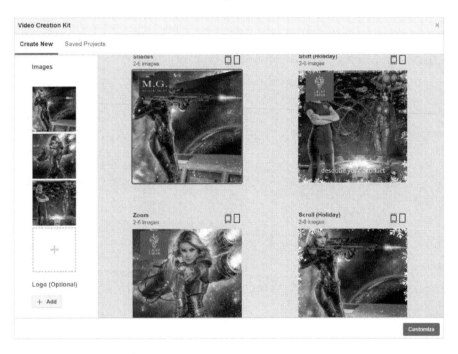

Here, you can see the video with a transform effect sliding into the next image in the sequence. In essence, these are really just spiffy slideshows, but they can make stills you have much more dynamic.

THE ANATOMY OF THE VIDEO AD

The ad itself is very straightforward, almost identical to a single-image ad once you get the video in place. You'll find the same fields and the same sorts of preview options.

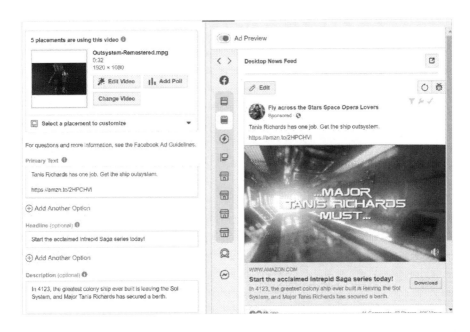

Like with images, Facebook now prefers video to be square or 4:5 ratio. The video I have in this example is 16:9 (standard HD resolution). It works OK, but on mobile, I get less of the screen—as you can see in the screenshot below.

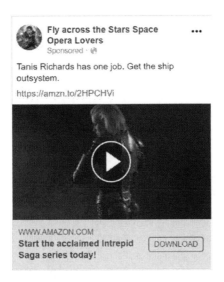

If this video were 4:5, it would use a lot more of the screen real estate. I've attempted to highlight this with the overlapping images below.

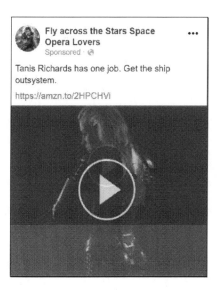

You'll note that I also went with shorter text in the description above this video because I want the user to focus on the video. I do this because I care about how long people watch the video for, and I don't want it to be because they're reading text.

Facebook used to recommend that videos stay under 45 seconds, but now they recommend that they are under 15 seconds. The reason for this is twofold.

1. People have short attention spans. This means you want to try to be concise. Your video should really only have one sentence in it. The video above contains this: "In the year 4123, Major Tanis Richards has one job: get the ship Outsystem."

2. Until the video finishes playing, clicking on it pauses
    the video. Once it's done playing, this overlay appears.

You don't want someone to have to wait 45 seconds to
see the prompt to download. Yes, it is also in the CTA
box below, but the more access the user has to it, the
better.

I personally counteract this by adding a text link in the
description above. That way there are two prompts,
one above the video and one below, should they choose
to click while the video is still playing.

LOWER CPC AHEAD

What you are likely to find is that video ads get a low CPC.
This is because Facebook likes video, and also because there is
less video on the platform. They have made a lot of tools for
turning still images into videos, and they can work as well as
real videos, provided they're done well.

Keep in mind that a good video (as opposed to the tools for turning still images into video) with compelling graphics and good music can cost you $50-$100 on the low end. This is why I recommend not experimenting with video ads until you really have still-image ads nailed.

There is, however, an exception to this rule. I mean...there always is, right?

SOMETIMES, SIZE DOES MATTER

I couldn't resist, OK?

Something I have had moderate success with, and other authors have had great success with, is doing readings as video ads.

If you do a non-scheduled FB Live video, or upload a video of your own making, you can convert them into ads; some people have had great success doing this.

Now, this depends a lot on how good a reading you can do, and whether or not you are comfortable being in front of the camera—as well as have a good mic, etc....

PART 9: THE FACEBOOK PIXEL

2nd EDITION NOTE: Huzzah! This section is entirely new!

OK, folks, now we're getting serious. We're getting to the pixel, that mysterious beacon of power you have heard rumblings about, disturbances in the matrix, but you never knew what mystical things lay beyond its portal…so you were scared.

But fear no longer! I, Malorie, will show you the way.

Too much?

Seriously, though, this part is the good part. This is where it gets real.

Read on…if you dare!

WHAT THE FREAK *IS* THE "PIXEL"?

Simply put, the pixel is a tracking code you can use on your website that is very much the same as the Google Analytics tracking code. Facebook even has a nifty dashboard that will show you all sorts of data about who goes where on your site, and what they do there.

The neat thing about Facebook is that because people are logged into Facebook on their browser while surfing the internet, the pixel code can connect people visiting your website with actual user accounts on Facebook.

What that means is that you can show *specific* ads to people who have viewed *specific* pages on your website…or who have viewed a certain number of pages on your site, or spent a certain amount of time on your site.

I'll be digging into *how* to do this in the next section, but I want to excite the heck out of you so that you actually do this, and then reap the sweet, sweet rewards.

INSTALLING THE PIXEL

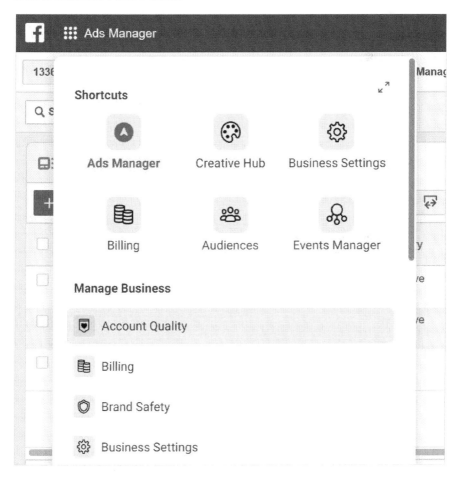

Inside the ads manager, click the little 9-dot menu thing (I have no idea what that's called), and when the menu opens, scroll down to "Events Manager".

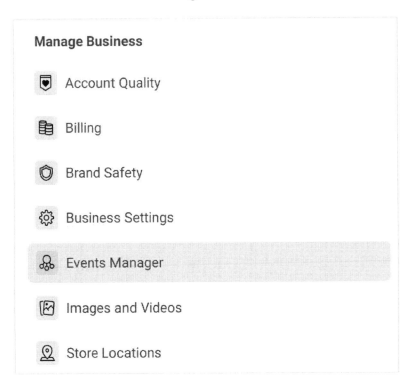

Once the page loads, you'll see an option to get started installing your Facebook Pixel.

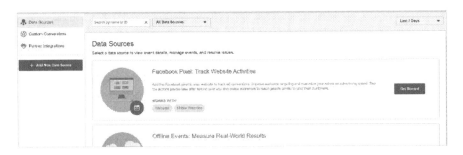

You'll be prompted to give your pixel a name (the default is fine) and then link a website, which you can leave blank.

On the next page, you'll see this pop-up:

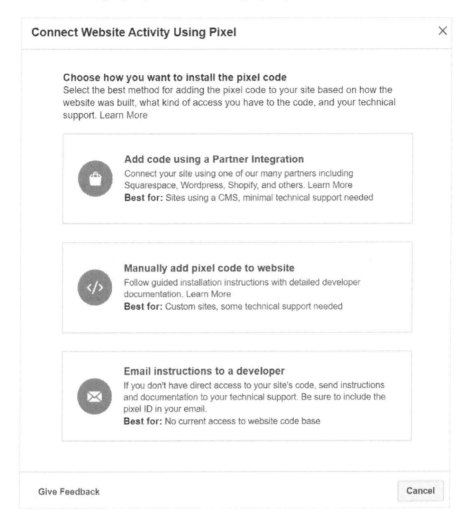

If you have Wordpress or a variety of other platforms, click the first option, and then choose your platform. Facebook has step-by-step guides for a variety of platforms.

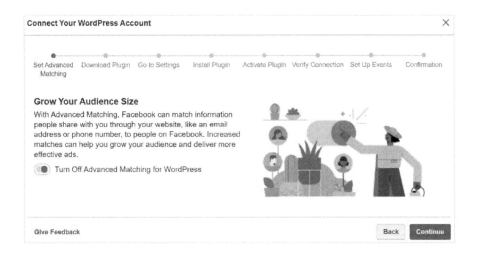

If you want to install the code manually, you can choose the second option and get the HTML/JS code to put on your site.

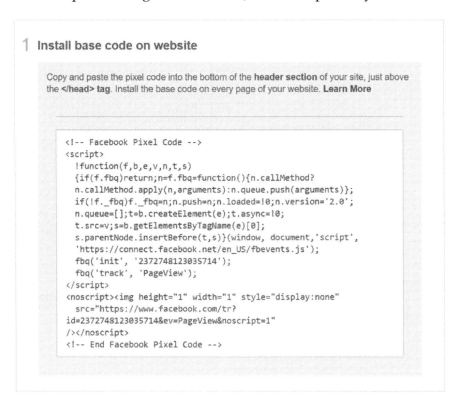

As an optional third method, you can look at this big block of code and see the "noscript" section at the bottom. If you grab the image tag in there, you can put that image into the footer of your site. It will be a 1px by 1px 'Pixel' (hence the name) that will be invisible.

```
<noscript><img height="1" width="1" style="display:none"
  src="https://www.facebook.com/tr?
id=2372748123035714&ev=PageView&noscript=1"
/></noscript>
```

<img height="1" width="1" style="display:none" src="https://www.facebook.com/tr?id=9923492308233233&ev= PageView"/>

You can remove the "&noscript=1" part.

Now, incidentally, my pixel ID is '9923492308233233'. Grab that, as you'll need it later. It can also be found elsewhere in the "Event Manager" interface.

Once the code is installed on your site, you can proceed to the next section.

CHECKING THAT IT'S WORKING

Go back to the menu and click "Analytics". Once that loads, you should see an option to select your Pixel.

NOTE: This can sometimes take an hour or so to show up.

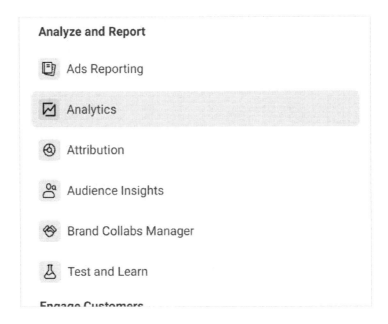

Click your Pixel name.

On the next page, you'll get a report of activity on your site that will show you who is going to it and what they're doing where. Analyzing this data for the purposes of improving your site could be a whole book, so we're simply looking to make sure that any data is showing up so that we know the pixel is working.

You'll find, as you look through the interface, that much of the data is the same as what you'll see in Google Analytics, or many other analytics tools, so few great insights are likely to appear as a result.

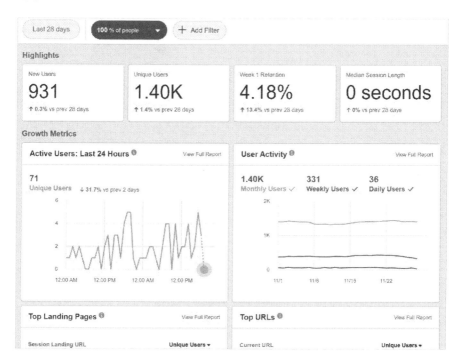

That's OK, though. That's not why we installed the mystical pixel.

Let us now ready ourselves to slay the great dragon known as *Retargeting!*

PART 10: RETARGETING

*2nd **EDITION NOTE:** This section is entirely new!*

I apologize for the last chapter. I'm doing final edits on this book the day after Thanksgiving, and clearly the turkey has been getting to me…

So, what is "Retargeting"?

Have you ever noticed that once you engage with a certain company online (such as liking one of their ads, or going to their website), their ads seem to follow you all over the Internet? They're doing that because it can take as many as 7-10 "touches" for a customer to buy something, and usually at *least* as few as 3.

I mentioned before that we'd like to think that the moment someone sees our brilliant ads, clicks through to witness the sheer genius of our blurb and mind-blowing cover art, that they'll instantly mash that "Buy Now" button and drop everything they're doing to read our book.

But they don't.

No, they're busy trying to get the kids ready for school, rushing to a meeting, trying to just chill out for a bit, stressed about a loved one who is going through a hard time, or maybe just searching for the right nacho dip.

That's why you'll need to reach them again. Remind them how awesome your book is. They'll get there, don't worry.

The way you do that is through retargeting them with ads that take them through a journey toward purchase.

In marketing, this is called a funnel. I'll talk a lot more about building a full marketing funnel in Jill's and my upcoming book on Marketing Strategies. Think of this section as work that will prime you for the big leagues.

Some of what I'll describe below, and what we'll teach in the marketing strategies book, comes from years of working on multi-million-dollar marketing campaigns that led customers through a funnel to an ultimate purchase and continued engagement (marketing-speak for "buying more of your stuff").

OK, so let's talk turkey…or rather, not turkey. We had enough semi-delirious, tryptophan-induced commentary in the prior chapter. Let's get to the details.

GETTING SITE TRAFFIC TO POPULATE YOUR PIXEL

Before we get to how to build audiences with the pixel, I should note that you do need traffic on your website to capture data with the pixel.

If your site isn't getting a hundred or more visitors a month, you might need to do some work to drive traffic there. An easy way to do that is by running ads on Pinterest. You can set a max bid of $0.10 per click there and drive 100 people a day to your site with a $10 budget.

Alternatively, you can have a lot of really awesome boards on Pinterest, where the pins link back to your pin pages. Other options include making your regular Facebook ads go to your website and require people to click "buy" links to go to the retailers.

Those options will also get you traffic that you can then use to retarget, and isn't a terrible idea for the purposes of feeding those people more ads.

Ideally, Amazon (*cough cough* If you're reading this, Amazon rep, listen up) would let us put the pixel, or some other conversion-tracking code, on our product pages so that we could tell who bought and who didn't. Then we could retarget the folks who did *not* buy after visiting our site.

Other systems let us do this, and I'll talk about them later.

A final method to get some more traffic to your site is to do some giveaways that require people to go to your site to take various actions (like get the book).

NOTE: Readerlinks.com also supports the Facebook pixel. If you utilize their book links system, you can plug in your pixel ID and then when people redirect through their system, you'll be able to track and retarget those buyers with more ads.

This is gold and saves you from doing any legwork.

BUILD AUDIENCES WITH YOUR PIXEL

When building an audience, you have few ways to go about it. Thus far, I've mostly focused on building with interests, but now we're going to toss that to the wind and dive into the custom audience.

First, we need to make a new Ad Set (in a new campaign or an existing one, either works), and under the "Audience" section, pick "Create New" and choose "Custom Audience".

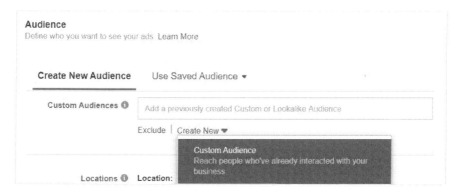

That will open a new window, where we choose "Website" as our source.

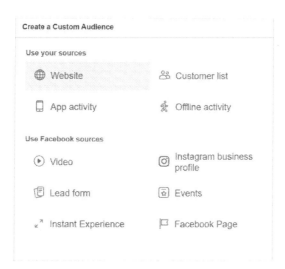

The simplest option is to pick all the people who visited your website in the past 30 days. I get about 1200-1800 people on my site when I'm not pushing any traffic to it, so I can drill down if I want; if you only have a few hundred, you might want to pick them all, like the default shows.

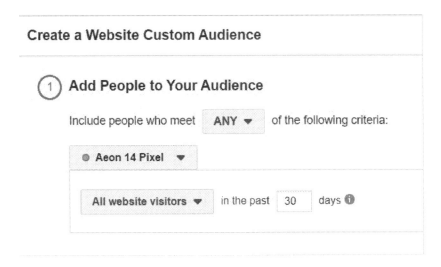

However, say you ran a promotion that sent people to a specific page. You might want to retarget people who just went to that URL.

Alternatively, you can also target the top 25% of people by time spent. This means the folks who spent the most time on your site. By nature, these folks showed the most interest in what you have to offer. You can also refine it by a specific book's URL and then market that book to them, or if it's in a series, market book 2 in that series.

Some special targeting I do is I run ads in print magazines. Those ads give links to specific URLs (in text and with QR codes), and then I run ads that specifically target those visitors.

I do the same thing at signings and shows. The cards I hand out often have special URLs, and when people visit those URLs, I feed them more ads to keep my books at the top of their mind.

Once you've made this new audience, you can make an ad for it, or use that audience to create a larger lookalike audience. This sort of lookalike has worked very well for me, as I can pump in all the people who visited my site in the past year (often in the tens of thousands), and build massive, very well-targeted lookalike audiences from them—especially when I pick people who spend the most time on my site.

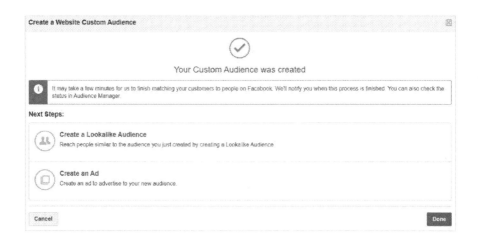

To carry on with the ad set we were making, click "Done" and carry on as usual. You're all set!

NOTE: Don't run huge budgets on these ads if you have lower site traffic and smaller audiences. Use these special audiences for special targeted ads, or low budget trickle ads.

VIDEO RETARGETING

Now, let's take those video ads you made that might only get a bit of clickthrough (as compared to regular single-image ads) and make them do double duty!

First, you need to let them run for at least a week or two to get some action before you start building audiences off them. We start the same way as we did with our pixel audience—by making a custom audience—but this time, we pick "Video" as our source.

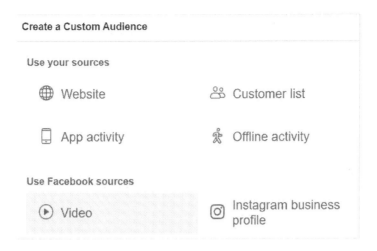

Once you do, you'll pick how much of your video they need to have watched. The longer they watched, the more engaged they are, but you might have a smaller group to target, so adjust as needed.

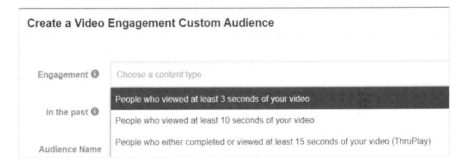

Once you make your selection, then you can pick the videos.

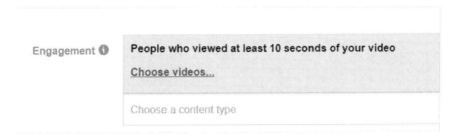

Despite what you pick, it only shows the number of people who watched for 3 seconds. Still, it's a gauge.

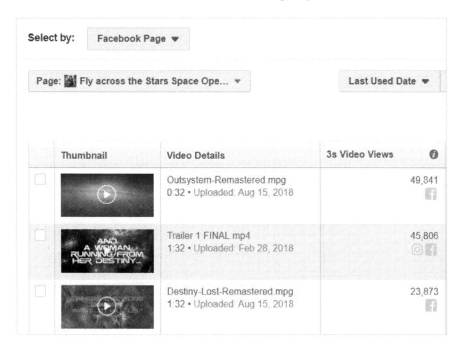

You can combine multiple videos, though, so that helps if you don't have a lot of views on individual videos.

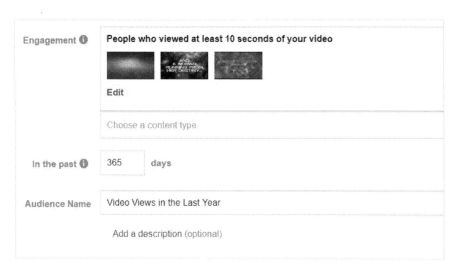

Then you're all set. Save your audience, and you can now use it.

INSTAGRAM RETARGETING

In Part 11 we talk about converting your Instagram account to a business account and then connecting it to your Facebook Author Page. Chances are you've already done that, but if not, you'll need to skip ahead to the Instagram section to learn how.

Well, well, well, now let's make that Insta action do double duty!

Back to our "Custom Audiences", and this time, pick "Instagram Business Profile".

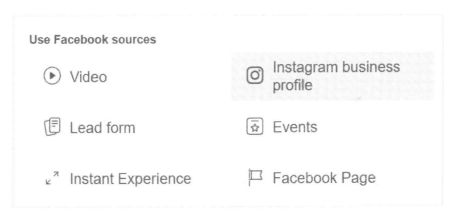

Some of these options are great! Look at that third one: "People who engaged with any post or ad". That means if you had a bomb-ass post that got 1000 likes, you can now show those 1000 users ads!

This stuff is gold.

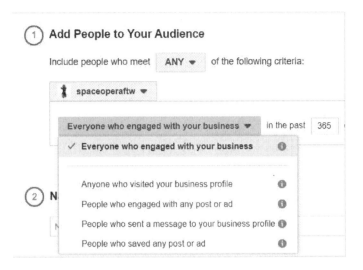

Once you select the option and save it, you can continue creating the ad set as normal.

FACEBOOK AD RETARGETING (WHAT, OMG!)

This one isn't immediately apparent, but since you run ads as your "Facebook Page", that's where the retargeting options live for creating audiences of people who engage with your ads on Facebook.

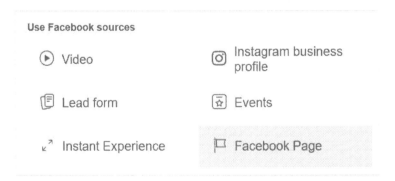

Alas, we can't target people who liked specific ads (which is where using the pixel can be a better option, in combination with sending people to your site, or using Readerlinks to identify people who are interested in specific books).

The options are very similar to the Instagram set, with the addition of people who clicked the CTA (the Call to Action, such as "Download" or "Learn More") on your ad.

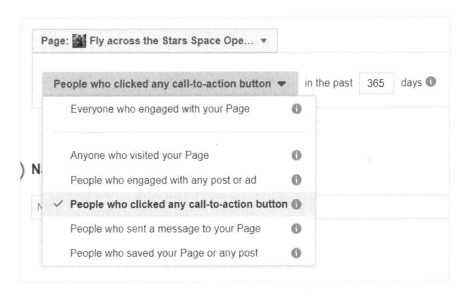

Just like the prior examples, make your choice, save the audience, and you can now proceed as usual.

EMAIL MARKETING RETARGETING

At this point, I think you're getting the hang of what is going on, so this is more of just a note about something that might seem obvious, but could be overlooked. It has three facets.

GAUGE ENGAGEMENT
The first is to periodically run offers that you send in your newsletter that require them to go to your website— preferably sending them to a specific URL that you can target.

A great thing would be a link to a freebie, or maybe a contest. Then you can make ads (preferably impression ads for these, not link click ads) that remind them about the contest, and even encourage sharing.

RETARGET UNOPENS

What is this sorcery? Burn it with fire!

Most email platforms will allow you to identify people who don't open, and many of us (including you, I hope) prune people who have not opened one of the last 6 or so emails off our lists so that we don't have to keep paying for them.

Thing is, we all feel some amount of angst about this. I mean, we *know* they were interested enough at some point to get on our list. We also know that they often don't open because of spam filters or some other deliverability reason.

Well, here's how you get a little bit more life out of them.

Export that list, and then go back to our friend, the custom audience builder. This time, pick "Customer List".

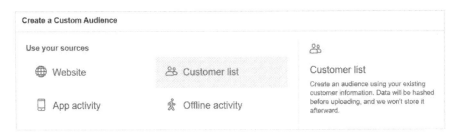

I'm not going to get into the details of what LTV is, so pick the option without it, "Use a file that doesn't include LTV".

Typically, we've scrubbed these people from our mail program, so I'll focus on the CSV-list version and not the Mailchimp option.

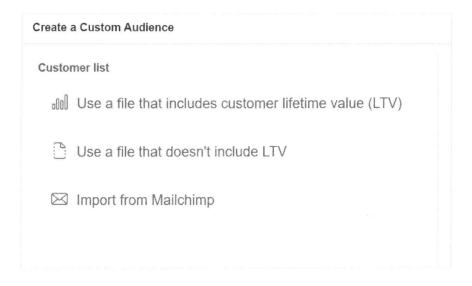

IMPORTANT. PLEASE READ.

Importing email addresses from your mailing list into Facebook *requires* you to have informed people when they signed up as to what types of services and 3rd-party sites you might share their information with.

The specifics of this depend on jurisdiction, with folks in the EU under the strictest requirements vis-à-vis GDPR. So long as your privacy disclosure that your sign-up form links to states that you may use data they provide in 3rd-party advertising platforms, you should be safe. I don't *think* you need to specifically name the platforms, but you might want to consult the specific regulations you operate under.

Facebook will require you to acknowledge that you have the requisite permissions upload your emails with the next screen, which, at the time of this writing, looks like this:

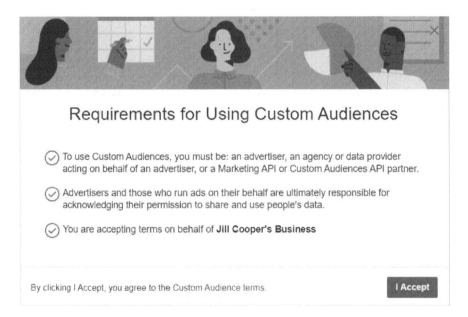

Also note, it is risky business to use unsubscribed email addresses here. It's not always illegal (depending on your jurisdiction), but it's at least bad mojo.

Upload your list, and then on the next page, you can do column matching.

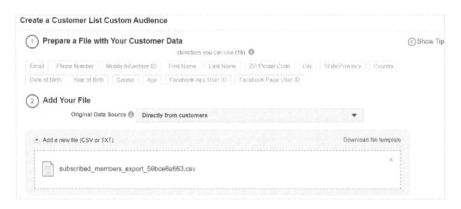

Not all of the columns can be matched, but usually Email, First, Last, and Country can be.

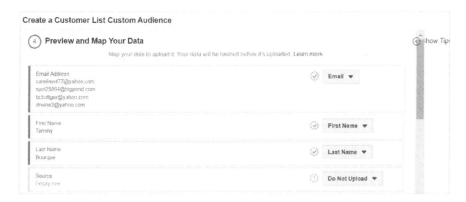

Once you upload the list, it will take about 30 minutes before Facebook completes the matching and gives you accurate audience counts, but otherwise, it's good to go!

Now you can target people who haven't opened the past few emails, and promote a special offer to them!

RETARGET PEOPLE WHO *DO* OPEN

Remember when I showed you the <IMG /> tag for your Facebook pixel on the Pixel install instructions?

<img height="1" width="1"
style="display:none"
src="https://www.facebook.com/tr?id=992
3492308233233&ev=PageView"/>

REMEMBER, THIS IS MY FB PIXEL ID. USE YOURS ;)

Well, we can put that in our email footer as well. In addition, you'll see that the event being tracked is "PageView". Well, that's not handy because we want to track email opens. In fact, all you need to do is change "PageView" to "EmailOpen"

```
<img height="1" width="1"
style="display:none"
src="https://www.facebook.com/tr?id=XXX
XXXXXXXX&ev=EmailOpen"/>
```

Again, remember to put in your FB Pixel ID, not mine.

Now, put that into the footer of your email, and once emails start getting opened, you're going to have a new option when creating custom audiences. Let's take a look at it!

Back inside Ad Set creation, let's make another Custom Audience. Once again, we choose "Website", as this gets us pixel data goodness.

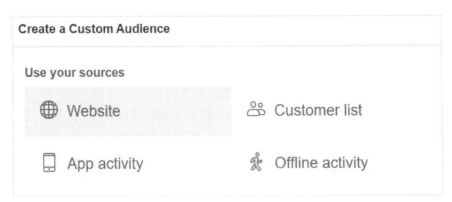

Once the event starts populating, you'll see a second option in your website activity dropdown! Now you can either create ads that target people who opened emails in the past X days, or even *exclude* them so that you don't pay for clicks or impressions for people who are already engaging with you.

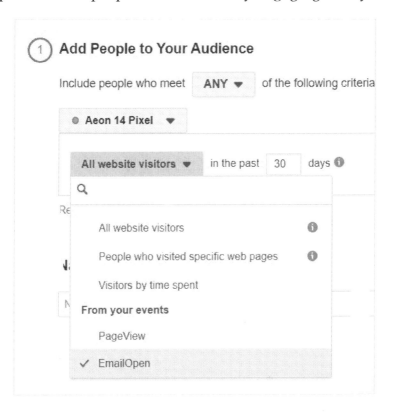

Once you pick the "EmailOpen" option, finish creating your custom audience, and proceed as normal.

BOOKFUNNEL FREEBIE SIGN-UP RETARGETING

One of the great sorrows of everyone who sells books is that it is very, very hard to track conversions. In marketing, a conversion is where we do a form of outreach, and then the people we are marketing to take the desired action.

Typically, that action is a sale, but it can also be an email list sign-up, or a download of a freebie on Bookfunnel. This is possible because the good folks at BF have made it so that we can add our Facebook Pixels to the landing pages we make there.

When editing or creating a giveaway page, down at the bottom is an "Advanced Settings" section.

When expanding it, we'll see a box for our Facebook Pixel ID and then two events.

The first event is what will get logged when the user loads the BookFunnel page to view your offer. The second event is what is logged when the user completes the required action to download your freebie (which might be nothing, or subscribing to your mailing list).

I bet you can see the options here. You can make audiences of people that view your Bookfunnel pages, but don't have a CompleteRegistration event logged.

Note: These events will show up in the same place as the EmailOpen event I showed you previously.

RETARGETING RETARGETING

I suspect that you can see how we're getting into building a funnel. This is a topic for its own book, but also something you can start thinking about now. How you could take people that you first reached with an email campaign or a Pinterest ad, funnel them to your website, then to a Bookfunnel freebie, and then begin to serve them ads for book 1 in your series (assuming the freebie was a prequel).

This sort of thing is what seasoned marketers really think about when they think of a "Campaign". It's a series of events that drive you ever closer to your goal.

Start with a campaign and call it "Outreach".

AD SET ONE

The first ad set targets people who came in from Pinterest (or links from forums, blog tours, what have you). You serve them a video ad on Facebook, and perhaps a still ad on Instagram.

AD SET TWO

Then you build audiences of people who interacted with those ads and serve them an ad that has a harder sell in it, pushing them to the Amazon (or other retailer) page to make a purchase.

AD SET THREE

At the same time, make an audience combining people from the first ad set, but who did *not* interact with the second set of ads. This can be a bit trickier to do, and only works well with video at present. as it's the only type of ad where we can specifically target an ad versus "any interaction".

However, you could make an audience of people who interacted in any way with your page in the past X days, and exclude them from this new audience.

Keep this audience set and use it for when you have sales, or for engagement campaigns that are more focused on reminding people that you exist and are less focused on the hard sell.

There you have it! A campaign with a 4-step funnel that moves people toward getting to your retail page and making a purchase!

But first, one final note:

DON'T FLOOD PEOPLE

When doing retargeting marketing, you need to remember that flooding people with your ads starts to feel like stalking. You need to give them a breather.

You want *"Oh, I remember that book, maybe I'll take a look."* Not *"Dear god, not this again, how do I stop seeing this ad everywhere! It's creepy!"*

Well, you're in luck! Facebook has a way to do that in at least a few scenarios.

Let's take the "10- Second Video Views" audience I made. I am going to make still-image ads that target people who have seen one of my video ads in the past year. However, some of those people will have just seen that ad in the past few days. I want to exclude them.

To do that, I make a *new* audience of people who have watched my video in the past 4 days, and then use it as my "Exclude" condition.

You can do this with Instagram audiences, website, Bookfunnel's pixel audiences, basically any option on the custom audiences source list.

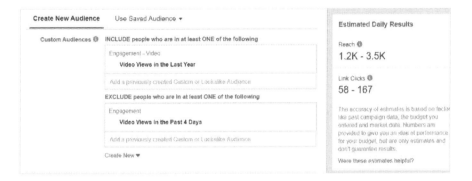

Another option is to exclude people who like your page, or have already clicked on other ads within the last 4 days. This will help you spend money on reaching new eyeballs, not hitting the same people over and over with the same ads.

PART 11: INSTAGRAM ADS

2nd EDITION NOTE: This section is entirely new!

Instagram is one of the most popular social media platforms out there, and since it is owned by Facebook, you can run your ads on Insta as well as on Facebook.

Back when I wrote the first edition of this book, you couldn't have clickable CTAs on Instagram, so ads there were more about awareness than conversions.

That has since changed, and now if you upgrade your Insta account to business, you can run ads there and have "Buy Now" buttons on them. To gain access to this, you must convert your Instagram account to a business one. You can do this in the Instagram app and then link it to a page on Facebook (you only need to do this if you want to make Instagram ads from Facebook).

First tap the menu on your profile page (the three horizontal lines in the upper right) to open the main menu. Then click the gear icon at the bottom.

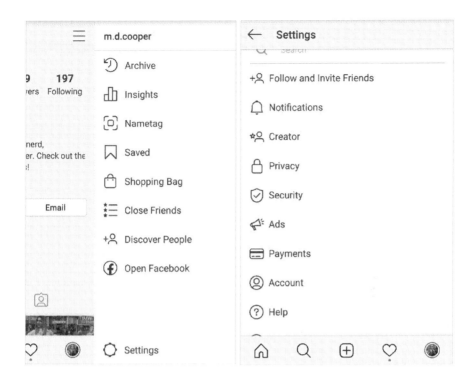

Then click the "Account" option and on the next screen, scroll to the bottom and you'll see a link to convert to a business account.

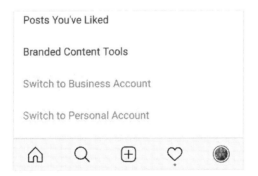

In my experience, converting to a business account does seem to limit the organic reach of posts you make on Insta, but at present, my experiences with that are anecdotal. Either way, you need to convert to either a business or a creator account on Instagram to run ads.

To be honest, one could write a whole book on Instagram ads, but in the interest of getting this book out on time, I'm going to focus on creating Insta ads from within the Facebook Ads Manager.

However, it is also possible to create posts within the Instagram app and then turn them into ads. There are arguments for each approach.

The number one reason you might want to create an ad from within the Insta app (called a "promotion" there) is that you can take an existing Instagram post and get more activity on it.

Promotions within Insta are very much like Boosted Posts on Facebook. Because these are existing posts, they continue to show in your grid of images on your profile page.

When you create Instagram ads within Facebook, they *don't* show up on your profile page on Insta, or anywhere else you can find (other than looking at your likes) for that matter.

Not having your ads show on your Insta profile might be something you want, because, let's face it, we all want a sweet-looking nine-grid, and ads made in Facebook's Ad Manager won't mess that up.

MIXING PLATFORMS

By default, Facebook is going to suggest you show the same ad on Insta and Facebook. This is something you pick when making an Ad Set, and it is called the "Placement".

Placement

◯ **Automatic Placements (Recommended)**

Use automatic placements to maximize your budget and help show your ads to more people. Facebook's delivery system will allocate your ad set's budget across multiple placements based on where they're likely to perform best. Learn More

● **Edit Placements**

Manually choose the places to show your ad. The more placements you select, the more opportunities you'll have to reach your target audience and achieve your business goals. Learn More

I recommend against running the same ad set on both Facebook and Instagram. Instead what I suggest is running separate ads and ad sets on both, and I have a good reason why: hashtags.

Devices

All devices

Platforms

☐ Facebook   ☐ Instagram

☑ Audience Network   ☐ Messenger

Asset Customization ℹ️

9 / 14 placements that support asset customization

Select All

Hashtags are very valuable on Instagram, but not particularly useful on Facebook. However, if you run the same ads on both platforms, you'll end up with a big block of thirty hashtags on your ads on Facebook, and that will just look weird.

Also, the formatting in posts, and even the type of content you put on Instagram, is different than Facebook, so you need custom ads to reach those users in the best way possible.

THE INSTAGRAM AD

So, what is different on Insta?

This is a bit counterintuitive, but unless you're posting something sexy, what people really like to see on Instagram are catchy images with long copy. Those convert the best and get the best engagement.

This is the very antithesis of the shorter, snappy ad copy people normally think about writing for ads.

In this particular case, the ad copy I wrote for Facebook was very personal and already fit well for Insta. It was conversational and seemed to get good engagement there.

Instagram ads also let you provide up to five options for description text, and it will select the best one. There is a text box for the headline, but I believe this is just a holdover from the Facebook ads interface, as there is no place a headline sections shows on Insta.

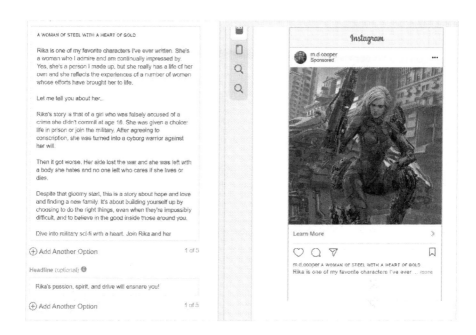

Sometimes I add my hashtags to the ad, and sometimes I add them in as a comment. I haven't been able to discern yet whether or not one works better than the other.

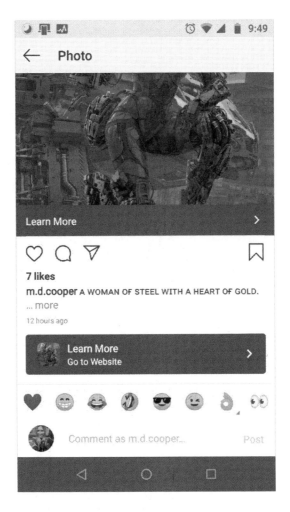

(What an Instagram ad looks like in the mobile app)

In all honesty, Insta ads are pretty straightforward, with the key there being an image that stands out in people's feeds, and a good use of hashtags, as well as a solid audience.

INSTAGRAM STORIES

Stories are another place your ad can appear, and these are nice because when they come up, they sit in front of the viewer for longer, and that's a great thing!

174

Keep in mind that if you decide to use the Instagram stories placement, you might want to jazz up the image yourself before posting it, because you won't have the story tool in Insta to make it swanky.

The dimensions for an Instagram story are 1080 x 1920. This is basically HDTV (1080p) turned sideways.

(May look a bit wider on the page here than it will be online)

There are myriad apps for spicing up an image, I did the following in Photoshop. Nothing excessive, just enough to make the image look more like a story that someone would have posted normally through the Instagram app on their phone.

Remember, that's what you really want on social media: content that blends in and looks like it belongs in the user's feed, not an interruption that looks like a hard-selling ad.

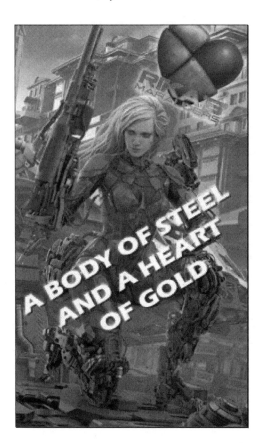

In Instagram, there will be an up arrow at the bottom with "Learn More" (or whatever CTA you picked when making the ad), and that is how people will engage with the ad and go to the destination you set.

Keep in mind that while you can do well with Instagram ads, the platform has less of a "buyer" mentality, and you'll find (on average) slightly lower conversions than with Facebook.

That being said, once you've built up a following there, it is a very good platform for getting engagement and interacting with existing readers.

PART 12: BOOSTED POSTS

2nd EDITION NOTE: This section is largely unchanged from the first edition (barring some edits for clarity). My opinions on Boosted Posts still stand.

It would be remiss of me not to discuss boosted posts, as they are a great way to engage with your readers, but they are less effective at general advertising.

They're great for engaging with your readers, because you want them to know about new books coming out, new deals, promotions, upcoming books, etc... And all that works best when it comes right from you, in a very conversational voice.

Also, your readers know where to go to pick up your books, so your calls to action (CTAs) can be simple links at the bottom of the post.

One thing I must, once again, state as strongly as possible: unless you're doing a cover reveal, the same image logic applies. Facebook will greatly prefer posts where the main image has no text.

I recently did a number of head-to-head tests on one of my fan pages, where I promoted a number of books for other authors. I did three with stock photos I picked up, and three with the book covers.

Facebook showed the ones with the stock photos 1500 times each. The ones that were just the book cover only got shown 300-400 times.

That's right: some of those posts reached 1/5 the people, just because I was lazy and didn't use a good picture. If ten of those missed 1200 people had bought the first book in a 5-book series, we know that the author missed out on at least $100 in read-through revenue. I later re-posted with better images.

"So why don't they work as well for general ads? They're awesome when I focus on my fans and their friends!"

The main reason is that there is no clear CTA (call to action), and that the image does not go to your destination.

Pretty simple, right?

On a purpose-built ad, the little link name in the lower left (usually AMAZON.COM), the CTA button on the lower right, *and* your image all go to your desired destination.

The Lost Colony Ship

In the spirit of great Space Opera by Peter F Hamilton, Jack Campbell, and Larry Niven comes Aeon 14. If you love strong heroines like Kris Longknife, then you're going to love Tanis Richards. Major Richards needs to get out of the Sol...

AMAZON.COM   Learn More

On a boosted post, clicking on the image just makes the image bigger. Your call to action is buried somewhere in your text, and looks like a link (and may look like a *messy* link), not a nice phrase.

Considering that there is nothing you can't do in an ad that a boosted post offers, I strongly suggest that you always do a regular ad when you're doing anything other than talking directly to your fans about some news or offer.

AN OFFER FROM THE WRITING WIVES

Over the prior two years, many authors have reached out to us to get help with ads and other marketing tasks. We have taken some ad-hoc engagements here and there, but have decided that we want to formalize what we have to offer to other authors who would like a hand.

We have a new website up at www.thewritingwives.com, where you can see what books we have out and also check out some of our new services. You can also learn about the writing retreats we're running!

The two services we offer at present are Ad Consulting and Blurb writing.

AD CONSULTING
You probably have a good idea whether or not we know anything about ads by this point. We've run ads across multiple genres and budgets, and can help you get your ads off the ground.

BLURBS
The other thing that we have a high level of experience and expertise in is blurb writing. Together, we've written over three hundred blurbs for our own books, hundreds of descriptions for our ads, and hundreds more of both for other authors. I don't think it would be an exaggeration at all to say that we've done well over a thousand blurbs and descriptions.

In the week before finishing this book, Mal did seven different blurbs. Some straight-up blurb creation, and others that were guided instruction to teach authors how to craft better blurbs.

This is an area that not only are we good at, but we actually *love* doing.

Visit www.thewritingwives.com/services to learn more about what we can do to help you.

BOOKKEEPING

Lastly, if you are dreading the end of the year, and the taxes that come with running a small business, Jill has begun leveraging her bookkeeping knowledge, and has packages to help authors with both year-end and ongoing bookkeeping. Check out what she has here:

https://www.novelbookkeepingsolutions.com

FINAL WORDS

There you have it: how to make some ads, and make some money on them—or at the very least, not lose too much money while you determine what works and what doesn't.

Advertising is one of the oldest things around, but it's not solved. No one has all the answers, and it's constantly changing. Don't beat yourself up if you don't nail it the first time out.

But know your baseline thresholds, the max CPC you can tolerate, the base relevancy/engagement you should shoot for, and the number of clicks to get a sale.

Some good baselines are:

- Keep it under $0.30 cost per click (CPC)
- Relevancy of at least 8 (or Average/Above Average) on the new engagement metrics.
- Shoot for *at least* one sale for every 30 clicks.

Remember, at $0.30 per click, and 30 clicks per sale, you're looking at $9 per sale, which means just one sale every two days (give or take a bit) when you're spending $5/day. However, in a series of books that have KU reads, that can be made back at around books 3 and 4 in the series.

That is also just a general threshold for what you want to shoot for. Your specific tolerances and measures for success will vary, but you **must** know what they are. And fail fast. Kill those bad ads in a day or two, not a week or two; tweak 'em, and make FB ads make you money!

NON-FICTION BOOKS BY JILL & MAL

HELP! I'M AN AUTHOR SERIES

Help! My Facebook Ads Suck *Second Edition*

Help! My Launch Plan Sucks

Help! My Marketing Strategies Suck

THANK YOU

Thanks for taking the time to read this book. We really do hope it helps you out on your journey as an author.

As you all know, reviews are the best social proof a book can have, and we would greatly appreciate your review on this one.

Also, if you got the free version of this book and would like to send us something in compensation, you can do so via PayPal here: http://paypal.me/woodenpenpress.

The Writing Wives,
Jill & Mal Cooper

Made in the USA
Columbia, SC
08 April 2021

35855282R00100